Rumours of Life

Rumours of Life

Reflections on the Resurrection Appearances

DAVID RUNCORN

DARTON · LONGMAN + TODD

This edition published in 1996 by
Darton, Longman and Todd Ltd
1 Spencer Court
140–142 Wandsworth High Street
London SW18 4JJ

ISBN 0–232–52088–7

A catalogue record for this book is available
from the British Library

Scripture quotations are taken from *The New International Version* published and copyright 1973, 1978 and 1984 by International Bible Society, and the New Jerusalem Bible, published and copyright 1985 by Darton, Longman and Todd Ltd and Doubleday & Co. Inc.

Thanks are due to Macmillan General Books for permission to quote copyright material from 'The Waiting' from *Later Poems* by R. S. Thomas.

Phototypeset in 11/13½ Raleigh by Intype London Ltd
Printed and bound in Great Britain
by Redwood Books, Trowbridge

To Jackie
whose word I believed

Contents

Acknowledgments   ix

Introduction   1

1 **A door has cracked open**   5
  The empty tomb

2 **Loving the space between**   18
  The risen absence of Jesus

3 **Why are you weeping?**   28
  Mary at the tomb

4 **Stranger on the road**   41
  The walk to Emmaus

5 **Some of our women amazed us**   56
  Women, men and the subversiveness of
  resurrection

6 **It's flesh I'm talking about here!**   71
The resurrection of the body

7 **The wounds that keep us**   84
The risen presence of Jesus

8 **The marks of believing**   97
Jesus and Thomas

9 **The far side**   110
The restoration of Peter

10 **What is that to you?**   123
A postscript

Notes   126

Acknowledgments

This book could only have been written with the support and encouragement of a great many people.

My thanks go first to Morag Reeve, my editor at DLT, for once again providing the encouragement and the opportunity to write.

The congregation of St Stephen's, West Ealing, give me time to write, and continue to be a wonderfully stimulating community in which to live, teach and preach. The Revd Mark Hargreaves and my wife, the Revd Jackie Searle, not only protected my space by kindly covering pastoral duties, but also read the text and made very helpful suggestions. Philip and Rosemary Young kindly gave me a room in their house in which to work. Simon Kingston once again gave generous time and help as the book evolved chapter by chapter.

This book was written during our son Joshua's first year of life. What he made of it I have no way of knowing, but I want to thank him for the delight of his distractions!

Introduction

I have a very clear picture of what a book on the resurrection is going to be like. The picture on the cover is a brilliant sunrise. The title and much of the text is emphasised with exclamation marks, and the book exudes energy and Christian confidence. I expect such a book to leave me feeling exhausted and very inadequate.

When I was writing *Touch Wood*[1] a few years ago, I planned to finish with a section on the resurrection. I looked forward to writing it. I felt I knew what I wanted to say, and was looking forward to saying it. Yet when I came to it, those chapters were the hardest part of the book. Once beyond the sunrises and the exclamation marks I made the painful discovery that I had little idea what I actually meant by the resurrection. The pages that I had expected to fill with stories of life and excitement lay blank for a long time. The message was clear: resurrection was not there for me to claim or use for my own ends.

I had to confess that I had been using the language of resurrection dishonestly. I realised I had been driving myself towards an elusive experience of Christ while the truth was actually something quite different. My own Christian experience was much more contradictory. And it was the same for most of my friends as well. I could not deny that I knew the love of Christ at work in my life, but there were times when I felt lost and confused, times when risen life seemed very far away. Like many people, I was trapped in an approach to Christian faith that vigorously proclaimed new life and urged me to forsake the old, but which wasn't very good at telling me how to get from one to the other. As most of us spend our lives 'in between', this wasn't very helpful.

I was reminded of a comment made by a woman who was put under great pressure in a Christian prayer group because the other members suspected she was not really filled with the Spirit and 'born again':

> Only men could speak about birth as if it were a quick thing, with an immediate change of 'before' and 'after'. Any woman knows that birth is long and slow, very painful and very messy. You expose the most embarassing parts of yourself and are so vulnerable that you are past caring. If that is what real birth is like, then why should spiritual birth be any different?[2]

That is why I have come to love this strange cluster of stories that we call the resurrection appearances. What we have here are not careful doctrinal statements about Christ, the Church and resurrection: we must turn elsewhere in the New Testament for those. We know the risen Christ taught the disciples, but his words and themes are scarcely reported at all. Raw shock and astonishment are the most vivid features of these accounts.

This is in marked contrast to the way the resurrection has been approached in recent years. It has become rather more an argument to be won than a place of wonder. Because traditional belief in the resurrection has been under theological attack, conservative Christian teaching has tended to feel on the defensive and has been concerned to verify its own position on the subject. That is not wrong, of course, but it is incomplete. The tomb is not simply there to be 'explained', as if establishing the *fact* were all that is needed.

Another tendency has been to start with the idea of 'resurrection' and to dip into the resurrection stories to illustrate the more general point that is being made. I think that misses the significance of these testimonies.

The gift of these brief, enigmatic, personal stories is to help us to understand the journey into new birth – of conversion to Christ. The first members of the Christian community were not ashamed to share the struggle involved in entering new life. Their turmoil and unbelief are recorded without excuse or self-justification. On this evidence, risen life is not for those who are ready to receive it. The only people in the Gospels to receive the resurrection were all totally and utterly *un*ready.

Christ comes to such people gently and with infinite care. He knows what his transforming life must ask of them. Ministering among them until his word and gift can be received, he guides them through the 'harrowing operation of conversion'.[3]

And so to this vulnerable and fallen world, now gloriously 'wounded by Grace',[4] the resurrection is not announced with deafening thunder or brilliant skies, but by a rumour – a rumour of life. 'Christ is risen'.

Easter Day

1 A door has cracked open
The empty tomb

'... there came a rich man from Arimathea, named Joseph, who had himself become a disciple of Jesus. Going to Pilate, he asked for Jesus' body, and Pilate ordered that it be given to him. Joseph took the body, wrapped it in a clean linen cloth, and placed it in his own new tomb that he had cut out of the rock. He rolled a big stone across the entrance to the tomb and went away.   (Matt. 27:57–60)

Most stories end at this point. This is where the Christian faith begins. Something happened in the night.

What God chooses to reveal or to keep secret is always a puzzle. A tomb left empty, the stone rolled away, waiting for someone to discover it, is a puzzling way to launch a new world. God has acted in the dark, when no one was around. No cameras were there to capture this unique and unrepeatable event. There were no press releases; no witnesses to question. Long before daybreak and the arrival of any human beings, without trumpets or loud announcements, God raised the dead and opened the tomb for all to see what he had done.

Traditional Christian teaching about the resurrection of Jesus has always insisted that the tomb was empty. Even while differing on other details, all four gospels agree on this fact.

The tomb itself was very public knowledge. It was owned by a prominent member of Jerusalem high society, Joseph of Arimathea (Matt. 27:57–60). His request to Pilate for the body was also very public – and in the circumstances courageous, even scandalous: he was offering to give his own tomb to a man condemned for blasphemy and executed as a common criminal. We know that the tomb was close to the place of crucifixion, and that it was located in a private garden (John 19:41–2). Joseph was assisted in the burial by Nicodemus, another prominent religious leader (John 19:39). Several witnesses watched them place the body of Jesus in the tomb and then seal it (Matt. 27:61; Luke 23:55). Short of putting actual directions to the tomb into their accounts, the gospels, taken together, could hardly have been more specific. In the small and intense world of Jerusalem society, the location of that unusual tomb would have been notoriously well known.

This was the tomb that was found empty, early on Easter morning. The stone had been rolled away. The body of Jesus was gone. There were angels around and the grave clothes had even been neatly folded. Are you surprised?

Absurd belief

'I believe that Christians need to recover a sense of the shocking absurdity of the very idea of resurrection,' writes Stephen Davis,[1] I think he is right. We know this story too well. We come to Easter morning like people reading a novel who have already read the last chapter and know how it all ends. The tomb has lost its power to surprise us.

No belief in the resurrection is complete without a sense of amazement and incredulity. It overwhelmed the life of the first Christian communities. 'The New Testament breathes an air of astonishment,' says Philip Seddon, 'the air of the first liberated people of creation, travellers emerging from a dark night into the brilliance of a long-awaited day, spellbound by God's inexpressible gift of himself'.[2]

My impression is that neither the liberal nor the Evangelical tradition copes well with the overwhelming mystery of what is found in the records of the first Easter. The former is embarrassed, uneasy with the idea of a dead body rising to life and sceptical of the historicity of the stories anyway, and prefers to retell the events as a *spiritual* truth. The latter vigorously defends belief in the empty tomb but tends to hide its unease by being aggressively factual.[3] The end result is the same, however: we end up with an Easter message that is credible and believable.

The first Easter was completely *un*believable. None

of the disciples came to believe in the resurrection of Jesus on the evidence of the tomb alone. Quite the reverse: it was a further tragedy. No one was expecting it. They were still traumatised by the events of the weekend, only to be plunged into further grief and confusion by what they saw. They appeared too dazed and helpless even to search the site or alert the authorities. That is what makes the abrupt (original) ending of Mark's gospel seem authentic. The impression he gives is that the ministry of angels only made things worse. Nothing could calm the disciples' terror. 'Trembling and bewildered, the women went out and fled from the tomb. They said nothing to anyone, because they were afraid' (Mark 16:8).

Coming to the tomb

The empty tomb has long held a fascination for me. Like the irresistible attraction on holiday of exploring caves in the cliffs, I find myself wanting to go in and explore. And that is precisely what we are meant to feel. The journey to the tomb is one that every believer has to make: it is there for *us* to discover, too. The tomb was not opened to let Jesus out – it was opened to let us in.

There is a need to recover the empty tomb as a place of spiritual pilgrimage and imaginative prayer. The Anglican communion liturgy thanks God who 'revealed the resurrection' (my italics) by raising Jesus to new life.[4] The phrase has always struck me as significant: it implies that the resurrection itself was never in doubt. God cannot die. But the surprise and gift of

Easter is that this resurrection is for us too. Jesus has been raised in our flesh and blood. It is our death that has been defeated.

In the church where I am vicar we have tried to give the empty tomb a more central place in the drama of our Easter worship. Late on Good Friday the altar becomes a tomb, surrounded in sacking, with an opening at the front. A large round 'stone' (made of papier maché) is placed across the entrance. There is a special service of lament, recalling the burial of Jesus.

On Easter Sunday the children roll the stone away, and look carefully to see whether there is anyone inside. All they find is some folded sheets. The whole service stops and we excitedly discuss what might have happened.

We find what Jesus often taught, that faith is awakened in the recovery of childlike wonder.

Death of death

There are those who claim that the empty tomb is itself irrelevant to the Easter message, and that attempts to make it a basis for faith are misguided. But its central place in the traditional Easter story is important. Not because it proves anything – it doesn't. It is significant for what it points to.

Firstly, the empty tomb reveals an act of God. The resurrection is first and foremost something that happened to Jesus, rather than something that happened to the disciples. Attempts to reinterpret the Easter story invariably place the emphasis on the latter, but it is highly questionable whether the disciples would have arrived at the idea of resurrection on their own. 'The disciples were prepared neither psychologically nor theologically for the idea of resurrection of a crucified messiah, and the fact that they arrived at this idea so early and confidently needs an explanation'.[5]

Secondly, the empty tomb witnesses to the physical resurrection of Jesus from the dead. This traditional belief has come in for heavy criticism from some modern theologians. The problem of empty tomb stories is solved by claiming that they were invented later to strengthen the Church's resurrection message.

There are no good reasons for suggesting this. For one thing it is hardly likely that a story written later would have included such specific, historical details. There would have been no point in including details that could easily be checked – not least the inclusion of a highly respected leader of Jewish society who was not known (until that point) to be a follower of Jesus. No one inventing the story would have chosen women as the first witnesses, either. None of the accounts reads like a later invention, nor has any attempt been made to smooth out confusing differences in detail between the gospels. They have all the vividness and clumsiness of eyewitness accounts. And the most likely explanation for including the otherwise irrelevant information about folded grave clothes, for example, is that this simply is an account of what Peter actually saw.[6]

Thirdly, the empty tomb connects the resurrection with the cross. The one who has risen is the same one who died. There is no room here for theories suggesting that the resurrection appearances involved some kind of substitution or mistaken identity. Moreover the witness of the tomb is confirmed by the wounds of crucifixion upon the risen Jesus. It is by those same wounds that the disciples fully recognised him (John 20:20).

Finally, the empty tomb separates Christian faith from spiritual theories of resurrection and ideas of the immortality of the soul. In my experience there are many Christians who hold to variations of this view under the mistaken impression that it is orthodox Christian teaching. The belief is that the human spirit is in some way 'naturally' eternal and continues life beyond physical death. Resurrection is the release of my spirit or soul into new life, 'liberated' from the constraints of my mortal body. Nowhere does the Bible teach this. On the contrary, the Christian hope of salvation is for the transformation of the body as well as of the spirit.[7]

> The Christian resurrection claim is an *empirical* claim: it entails the life after death of *living bodies* (although of a transformed sort) that can be seen and touched. The resurrection does not mean that, much to our pleasant surprise, we human beings turn out to have an indestructible aspect that survives death. It means rather that death has been defeated by a miraculous and decisive intervention by God.[8]

The open door

In Tom Stoppard's play *Arcadia*, Valentine explains, with growing excitement, the way that chaos theory has thrown the settled world of science into confusion. It has overturned the old order based on the binding predictability of Newtonian physics. The changes it is bringing are uncertain. But it promises, for Valentine, a revolution that is full of new life and vitality: it involves a radical transformation in the way that the world and all within it are understood. The change is so complete that it feels as if life itself is starting all over again. On the threshold of this new age he rejoices in language of exhilarating faith.

> 'It makes me so happy. To be at the beginning again, knowing almost nothing. The future is disorder. A door like this has cracked open five or six times since we got up on our hind legs. It's the best possible time to be alive, when almost everything you thought you knew is wrong.'[9]

His words bring to mind the picture of the empty tomb.

Risen indeed

Throughout the history of the Church the empty tomb has stood as a silent inspiration to Christians facing the most extreme persecution and suffering. The belief that death itself has been defeated makes faith and hope possible in otherwise impossible circumstances.

As a student in Moscow at the height of State persecution of Christians, Michael Bordeaux attended the Easter celebration at an Orthodox church. What he experienced there changed his life. He stood in the darkness and listened to the procession approaching the church, chanting the Easter liturgy. 'They have taken away my Lord and I do not know where they have laid him.' 'Whom seek ye?' 'The body of Jesus.' 'Why seek ye the living among the dead? He is not here. He is risen – *Khristos voskrese!*' In the darkness, the Paschal candle was lit.

In less than a minute five thousand individual flames united in one faith. Each candle lit up a face behind. That face bore the deep lines of sorrow, of personal tragedy. Yet, as it was illuminated, the suffering turned to joy, to the certain knowledge of the reality of the risen Lord.

Often since that Easter midnight have I reflected how that single five minutes of experience taught me the certainty of the resurrection in a way that reading a hundred theological books had not quite managed to do. 'How could they be so sure?' I asked myself. The answer always came back: they have trodden the way of the cross to the hill of Calvary. Their suffering under Stalin stripped them of every material advantage and reward; they were imprisoned; dear ones died in every family.

They do not debate the resurrection: they have experienced its reality in their own lives. They have not preserved the faith in hostile surroundings; it has preserved them. Their joy is truly a glimpse through the curtain which divides us from heaven.[10]

In 1977 Archbishop Janani Luwum was murdered in Uganda on the orders of President Idi Amin. Unlike Pilate, Amin refused to release his body for burial and banned any funeral gathering. In the grounds of the cathedral, however, the grave had already been dug, and thousands of people gathered there. Margaret Ford describes the unforgettable moment that followed:

> Our eyes fell on the empty grave, a gaping hole in the earth. The words of the angel to the two women seeking Jesus's body flashed into our minds. 'Why do you seek the living among the dead?' Namirembe Hill resounded with the song that the balokole ('the saved ones') have taken as their own:
>
> > Glory, glory, hallelujah,
> > Glory, glory to the Lamb!
> > Oh, the cleansing blood has reached me,
> > Glory, glory to the Lamb.
>
> We came away from the service praising, healed by the revelation of the empty grave.[11]

Upside-down believing

I once had a meeting with a couple who wanted a church wedding. As they had no Christian background, I started by telling them about Jesus and spoke of the cross and the resurrection. They were already looking bored. Then I said, 'Of course, if he rose from the dead then he's around now – he's here with us.' They reacted immediately. The groom only just resisted the urge to check whether anyone was behind the sofa. The bride went pale and admitted, 'It sounds a bit spooky.'[12] The incident shook me, too – I had not expected their surprise. I realised that I had ceased to speak of the resurrection with any sense of wonder. This is the peril of overfamiliarity. The truth is that

> the resurrection is not just a unique and improbable event but an intellectual scandal. It is the sort of event that conflicts so radically with so many well-established scientific laws that any attempt to revise them in such a way as to allow for resurrection would vitiate them.[13]

We should not be surprised that our modern world finds the idea of resurrection difficult or unacceptable. The world of the first disciples found it just as difficult. The gospels were not written to confirm any existing world view, but to challenge and transform it: 'these are written that you may believe that Jesus is the Christ, the Son of God, and that by believing you may have life in his name' (John 20:31).

In any age, believing the resurrection of Jesus requires what Charles Handy has called 'upside-down thinking'. He was writing about those times in history when an event or a series of events so contradicts what has gone before that it throws old ways of thinking and understanding into chaos. It requires new and unreasonable ways of thinking and acting to respond to it, 'even if both thinkers and thoughts appear absurd at first sight' (my italics).[14]

Handy believes that Western civilisation is in the midst of just such a time of critical change and that the outcome is not at all certain. If he is right then Christian faith is well equipped to live within such a world, for the resurrection is completely unreasonable. God has broken all the rules. The empty tomb is the ultimate act of what Handy calls 'discontinuous change'.

Resurrection life requires upside-down thinking, and the closer to the truth we get, the more we will also feel the absurdity of what we believe.

Among the dead

This struck me in a new way when I led a clergy quiet day at a retreat house in Essex a few years ago. It was shortly after Easter and I decided to speak on the resurrection stories. After the first address I encouraged the group to spend time alone imagining themselves among the first disciples on Easter day. The weather was warm and most people went into the large garden at the back of the building. Only a little later did I realise that the retreat house was one of the earliest Quaker meeting houses in the country. The garden was the resting place for early generations of Quaker families. Looking outside I found clergy sitting and lying among the gravestones, contemplating resurrection.

> In the morning,
> long after daybreak,
> we came to the garden
> and found a graveyard.
> No one had rolled
> away the stones.
>
> And standing forelorn
> among the tombs
> a child's climbing frame
> rusted,
> abandoned,

like a badly misjudged gift,
for who comes to play
at the mouth of the grave,
and do the dead need
recreation?

But *someone*'s weight
had bent those rungs.
Beside the stones we wondered.

There in the garden
which is a graveyard
and was a playground
began
(and not for the first time)
a rumour of angels
while somewhere near,
discreet,
not wishing to offend,
their laughter all above
our ears,
they played away that
long hot day,
just killing time
(which is their work)
and wondered that we sat
among the dead.[15]

2 Loving the space between
The risen absence of Jesus

Very early on the first day of the week, just after sunrise, they were on their way to the tomb and they asked each other, 'Who will roll the stone away from the entrance to the tomb?' But when they looked up, they saw that the stone, which was very large, had been rolled away. As they entered the tomb, they saw a young man . . . and they were alarmed. 'Don't be alarmed,' he said. 'You are looking for Jesus the Nazarene, who was crucified. He has risen! He is not here. See the place where they laid him.'　(Mark 16:2–6)

The first experience of resurrection for the disciples was not presence but absence. Jesus was gone and they didn't know where. While angels kept telling them what good news it was, the situation left them in turmoil. According to St Mark's gospel, the women found it all so terrifying that they fled from the tomb in fear and didn't tell anyone what they had seen (16:8).

In fact in the forty days that followed, Jesus seems to have been much more absent than present. We have records of up to eight appearances by Jesus (though it is impossible to be precise) and many of the encounters described were quite brief. This means that the disciples had a great deal of time between meetings with Jesus. The evidence of the resurrection stories is that Jesus gives his disciples a lot of space.

It is very curious that Jesus seems to spend so *little* time with his disciples. At such a critical time of preparation for the new age of the Church we might suppose that he would want to pack every risen day with training courses, retreats, leadership training, and workshops on healing and counselling. Instead all we have is a handful of unpredictable and enigmatic encounters with individuals or groups of disciples. While endless sermons and books are written on the resurrection *presence* of Jesus, his risen *absence* is almost totally ignored. The angels were quite clear – he is risen, he is *not* here. 'The risen Jesus' does not automatically mean 'the present Jesus'.

Divine absence

We start with a basic problem. A great deal of Christian believing has no positive understanding of God's absence at all. I don't mean that God is truly absent – I am thinking of those times when he seems to withdraw his presence and we cannot find him. He is not where we expected him to be. Then we tend to believe that it must be because we have done something wrong. We accuse ourselves: I'm not praying enough; I have sinned; God doesn't love me any more; he is teaching me a lesson. After all, hasn't he promised never to leave us?

I once found a friend of mine in a Christian bookshop buying an armful of books with such titles as *Restoring Your Spiritual Passion* and *Victorious Christian Living.* As we talked it became clear that he was in turmoil. A previously lively faith had gone totally dry on him. He was desperately looking for a way of recovering the old feeling. God seemed so far away; he was absent where he had always been present. I sat there listening, with the uncomfortable feeling that my friend had just wasted his money. The grace God was giving him was his absence, not his presence. And if that was where God wanted him, then no amount of spiritual reading would change that. He must learn to wait in the dark and the emptiness. Part of his pain was that nothing in his Christian life had prepared him for an absence of God that wasn't either the failure of faith or the death of it.

By contrast, the Eastern Orthodox churches have always understood the importance of divine absence. In a way that Western churches have neglected, the Orthodox tradition has always taught the importance of darkness, the desert and spiritual emptiness in the Christian experience. Metropolitan Anthony Bloom's classic book *School for Prayer*, for example, begins with a whole chapter on the absence of God. He insists that there are times when God withdraws his presence out of love and a desire to protect us. He reminds us

that every meeting with God is a moment of judgement
for us, for God is truth, holiness, power. We cannot
seek his presence lightly. His love is like a consuming
fire for us. So, says Metropolitan Anthony, we should
be thankful to God 'that he does not always present
himself to us when we wish to meet him, because we
might not be able to endure such a meeting'.[1]

The tyranny of presence

There can be in the Church a misplaced loyalty to
the *presence* of Christ which can be exhausting and
oppressive. Unless the presence of God is balanced
by a positive understanding of his absence then our
experience of God may become very destructive.

A few years ago I reached a personal crisis in my
life. At rock bottom and close to a breakdown, I was
near to giving up both my work and my faith. Friends
cared and prayed for me and I was genuinely grateful.
But I remember how often I heard people praying for
God's presence to be real to me. I didn't know how to
tell them that that was exactly what I *didn't* want. His
presence had become a total burden. I wanted his
absence. I wanted space.

But the Church is not the place you can say that sort
of thing – and especially not if you are a vicar! I needed
someone to pray: 'Lord, it gets a bit too much with
you around at times. You can be very demanding. David
needs a break. Stop trying to help. It just makes it
worse. Leave him alone for a bit and give him a rest.'

I took myself off to the Alps and spent two months
in a cabin on my own. Christian life for me had been

intensely about presence – the presence of God, of the Church, the world, my friends, my work. The experience was hard but life-changing.[2]

While I was away I came across this story in *Zorba the Greek*:

> I remembered one morning when I discovered a cocoon in the bark of a tree, just as the butterfly was making a hole in its case and preparing to come out. I waited a little while, but it was too long appearing and I was impatient.
>
> I bent over it and breathed on it to warm it. I warmed it as quickly as I could and the miracle began to happen before my eyes, faster than life. The case opened, the butterfly started slowly crawling out and I shall never forget my horror . . . when I saw how its wings were folded back and crumpled. The wretched butterfly tried with its whole trembling body to unfold them. Bending over it I tried to help it with my breath. In vain. It needed to be hatched out patiently and the unfolding of the wings would be a gradual process in the sun. Now it was too late. My breath had forced the butterfly to appear, all crumpled, before its time. It struggled desperately and, a few seconds later, died in the palm of my hand.[3]

Up there in my amateur hermitage, I remember weeping bitterly. My experience of Christianity had been just such a hot breath, a constant forcing before its time, a suffocating presence. My faith had all but died. If I was to know risen life, it would have to come another way.

Giving space

'Giving space' is not usually the way the Church describes its ministry. Nor is it the way many Christians would describe their own church life! We are usually preoccupied with getting people more involved. But in our enthusiasm it is perilously easy to force people to grow and respond at a pace we set for them. It seems that an important feature of resurrection life involves learning to live with space.

Puzzling over why many people are drawn to churches but stay on the edge, I have noticed how often they will complain of a time in their lives when they had God forced upon them. Sometimes, perhaps, it is just an excuse. But those who are trying to be honest have an important story to tell. The problem may have been well-intended pressure from parents, the dullness of compulsory school assembly, or a bad experience of church. But now, through no fault of their own, they have become unwilling to get too close to a God they sense as having violated their space, imposing his heavy presence with exhausting demands that lacked nurture, humour and love. There is often a deep weariness of spirit in such people, which is difficult to minister to.

'I know the answer's Jesus,' said a bored Sunday school child, asked to name an animal that lived in trees, ate acorns and had a long bushy tail, 'but it sounds awfully like a squirrel to me.' What some people need is the grace of God's absence. There are lessons of faith and awareness we only learn alone. Even God must withdraw from us.

An American priest with a busy national speaking ministry spoke of a time when he felt God tell him to keep every morning empty for the whole month leading up to Christmas. He described his struggles day by day. As the grip of his previous lifestyle began to lessen in the silence he came to look on his own ministry and life with new eyes. He saw that much of what he thought was 'spiritual' and important was actually his own ambition and refined showmanship. He called that whole time a process of drastic detoxification – from his own busyness, from his need for recognition and importance. He was being weaned off deep-seated addictions to religious activity, the obsessiveness that we so easily confuse with the real thing. And the grace of God's absence prepared him in a new way to be a minister of his presence.

Unmasking illusion

Anyone who has spent time in silent retreat will have known something of this struggle. Coming from very busy lives, we need time to stop and unwind and to become still. We come longing for space, but as the silence takes hold and stillness grows around us, the absence of people or things to do can become deeply unsettling. The temptation is to fill up the space. Anything will do. At such times the need to make coffee every half hour can have an almost demonic intensity.

In the space that is God's absence, our religious games are eventually seen in all their emptiness. Our false pictures of God and ourselves are exposed for what they are. Our ploys for trying to control God are uncovered. In the Bible the place of God's absence is the wilderness. It is the place where faith is purified and where the power of false gods is broken. It is for this reason that Thomas Merton, writing of the importance of solitude, described Christian prayer as 'the unmasking of illusion'.

Pastoral ministry is never more painful than at times like that, when you know that you can offer nothing to take away the pain of a person's journey through what feels like abandonment, desolation and emptiness. You can only affirm the absence as the risen absence of Christ. To be there is not a failure but a sign of grace. There is nothing else to do but wait in the dark. A superficial comfort at such a time, a spiritual Band-Aid, is no solution at all.

The space between

The simplest and most obvious thing that Jesus was teaching the disciples after the resurrection was how to have a living relationship with him. After all, the freedom to be absent from or present to someone is what makes real friendship possible. The truth is that any relationship based entirely on presence quickly becomes suffocating and oppressive. This is as true of our relating to God as of our relating to each other. Walker Percy was struggling with this when he wrote, with weary and characteristic bluntness:

Christ should leave us. He is too much with us and I don't like his friends. We have no hope of recovering

Christ until Christ leaves us. There is after all something worse than being God-forsaken. It is when God overstays his welcome and takes up with the wrong people.[4]

The ability to love another is not measured by how close we can get. It is actually about the freedom to give the right space. Too close, and our possessive clinging will choke all life out of our relationship. Too distant, and we will simply drift apart. In his beautiful meditation on marriage, Kahlil Gibran affirms all that unites a couple but urges, 'let there be spaces in your togetherness. And let the winds of the heavens dance between you ... Sing and dance together and be joyous, but let each one of you be alone.'[5]

The poet Rainer Rilke says the same thing more strongly. 'I hold this to be the highest task of a bond between two people: that each should stand guard over the solitude of the other.' They are to encourage each other's solitude and their times together are 'true sharings which interrupt periods of deep isolation'.[6] This sounds a complete contradiction alongside the popular understanding of loving. Love is surely about being together, not being apart? But in another place Rilke develops this idea more fully:

Togetherness between two human beings is an impossibility and, when it seems to occur, a limitation, a mutual compromise, which robs one side, or both, of their fullest freedom and development. But once the awareness is granted, that even between the closest of human beings there remains an infinite distance, then a wonderful living-alongside-each-other can spring up, when they succeed in loving the distance between, something that makes it possible for them to see each other in their wholeness and against the background of the vastness of heaven.[7]

The freedom to love

'He is *not* here.' Risen life means learning to live between the absence and the presence of Christ – and to love the space between. For the risen Jesus, Jesus the Lord, is an absence that is never abandonment and a presence that is not possession.

Jesus gives to his disciples the degree of space that makes real loving possible. And in that space we may freely learn to love him in a relationship that is as terrifying as it is glorious.

I have come to picture the absent Jesus, just out of sight of the disciples, yet present to all their fearful watching and waiting, quietly standing guard over their solitude.

3 Why are you weeping?
Mary at the tomb

Early on the first day of the week, while it was still dark, Mary Magdalene went to the tomb and saw that the stone had been removed from the entrance. So she came running to Simon Peter and the other disciple, the one Jesus loved, and said, 'They have taken the Lord out of the tomb, and we don't know where they have put him!'. . .

Mary stood outside the tomb crying. As she wept, she bent over to look into the tomb and saw two angels in white, seated where Jesus' body had been, one at the head and the other at the foot.

They asked her, 'Woman, why are you crying?'

'They have taken my Lord away,' she said, 'and I don't know where they have put him.' At this, she turned round and saw Jesus standing there, but she did not realise that it was Jesus.

'Woman,' he said, 'why are you crying? Who is it you are looking for?'

Thinking he was the gardener, she said, 'Sir, if you have carried him away, tell me where you have put him, and I will get him.'

Jesus said to her, 'Mary.'   (John 20:1–2, 11–16)

A woman comes to a tomb. This could be a scene from anywhere in the world.

But Mary is not coming to mourn at a grave-side. There is still work to be done: the burial of Jesus is not complete. In this culture the burial of the dead includes important rituals of anointing, and there has not been time to complete these before the start of the Sabbath. This explains the conversation recorded in Mark's gospel, where we read that Mary, in company with other women, is worried about how they are going to move the stone away from the entrance and get into the tomb (Mark 16:1–3).

Jesus was laid in a rich man's tomb, which would have been a family vault. The body would have been left in the small antechamber, waiting for final anointing and then burial in one of the smaller vaults hollowed out of the rock face at the back of the tomb.

When the women arrive they are astonished to find the tomb is already open – and empty! There is a burst of hectic activity. Peter and others come running to check. The body of Jesus is definitely not there. The shock and confusion are all described in a few short verses (John 20:1–8).

The story began with Mary, however, and it now returns to her. The other characters, the noise and excitement, all die away. We are left with Mary, alone outside the tomb. She is weeping.

This is a story about tears and resurrection.

The grace of tears

Mary weeps. That in itself is enviable – ours is not a culture that is comfortable with tears: we are trained out of them from our earliest years. We learn that we must keep them hidden. Crying is childish; it is a weakness. Weeping is a social embarrassment, and we speak of it as a kind of bodily malfunction: we call it 'breaking down'. We try to 'pull ourselves together' or 'get a grip on ourselves'. Time and again I have watched mourners at funerals struggling to hold back tears as if these were wrong or inappropriate. I have listened to people telling me the most harrowing stories and then apologise for their tears as if weeping were an indulgence. Tears are simply not very 'British' (and not very 'Church of England', either). They are to be kept firmly under control, and so our grief is repressed.

By contrast, the culture in which the Bible was written was much more open and relaxed about emotions in general. The people of the scriptures had no such inhibitions. Tears were 'allowed'. Tears guided the faithful through grief and struggle and renewed them in their pilgrimage. Many of the psalms reflect the paradoxical way in which tears both acknowledge our pain and death, and actually become the means by

which we enter the new life beyond. The acceptance
of death makes rebirth possible.

> Those who sow in tears
>   will reap with songs of joy.
> He who goes out weeping,
>   carrying the seed to sow,
> will return with songs of joy,
>   carrying the sheaves with him.
>
> (Ps. 126:5–6)

> Blessed are those . . .
>   whose hearts are set on pilgrimage.
> As they pass through the Valley of Tears
> they make there a water-hole,
> and – a further blessing! – early rain fills it.
>
> (Ps. 84:5–6 NJB: *alternative reading*
> *for 'Valley of the Balsam'*)

Jesus taught that grieving was a special gift. In the
Sermon on the Mount he pronounced a special blessing
on those who mourn. He himself is recorded as weeping and expressing deep emotion on many occasions,
and is remembered, in the words of Isaiah, as a 'man
of sorrows'. Tears often flowed in the gospels when
people met Jesus and experienced his love and healing.
In the very moving story of the prostitute who caused
a scandal by weeping over the feet of Jesus before
drying them with her hair, Jesus received her action as
an anointing (Luke 7:36–50).

What is less well known among Christians today is
the way the Church down the centuries has always
given special importance to tears in the spiritual life.

The presence of tears is a mark of grace. They have been seen as a sign of God's Spirit at work in the deep places of a Christian's life, releasing the believer to fresh repentance and renewed self-offering. The gift of tears is to be sought from God.

In the early centuries of the Church, the writings of the great spiritual teachers, such as Gregory Nazianzen, Ephraim the Syrian, John Climacus and Symeon the New Theologian, all included long discussions on the importance and discernment of tears in the Christian life. In the Western Catholic tradition, St Benedict put similar emphasis on it.

Long before the insights of modern psychology, these pastors understood the unique therapeutic power of tears in relating the unconscious and conscious parts of personality. Tears heal and strengthen the psychosomatic unity of a person. They are also a physical, bodily expression of a person's innermost spirit. But above all, tears are a profoundly important way in which the Holy Spirit works in the believer. For this reason tears have been spoken of as a continuation of our baptism, or a baptism of the Spirit.[1]

Neglected gift

In today's Church the Pentecostal and charismatic movements have liberated many people into a new emotional freedom in their Christian life and worship – and goodness knows we need it! Tears are very commonly experienced where there is new awareness of God's Spirit. Yet at such times weeping is too easily understood as a response to a spiritual 'crisis', or simply as a part of healing ministry. It may be both of those, of course. But there seems to be little awareness of the historic tradition in the Church within which this phenomenon stands. At the time of writing I know of hardly any teaching on tears in currently popular books on Christian prayer and theology.[2] All of which means that the stress of the earlier Church teachers on this unpredictable emotion can sound very strange to Western ears:

> give me the tears of penance, loving tears out of love, tears of salvation, tears that clean the darkness of my mind, making me light so that I may see You, Light of the world, Enlightenment to my repentant eyes.[3]

Isaac the Syrian believed that tears were one of the first signs of God's grace at work in a person:

> When grace has begun to open your eyes so that they perceive things by means of precise vision, at that time your eyes will begin to shed tears until they wash your cheeks by their very abundance. If any one teaches you otherwise, do not believe him. To ask of your body anything else apart from tears as an outward sign of reality, is not permitted to you.[4]

These were not the tears of a spiritual crisis or an emotional conversion experience. Isaac knew how to distinguish passing emotional moods from the presence of the Holy Spirit. He taught that tears were the truest measure of continued progress in the Christian life. To young monks he wrote:

I am going to tell you something at which you must not laugh; for I am telling you the truth. Though you should suspend yourself by your eyelids before God, do not imagine that you have attained anything in your rule of life until you encounter tears; for until then your hidden self is still in the service of the world.[5]

The taming of tears

My own pastoral and personal experience suggests that tears are *very* present in the lives of many people. But our social and spiritual inhibitions are deep and powerful and we do not know how to recognise or honour the tears. Emotion has long been confused with emotionalism, and we have forgotten how to tell the difference. Our culture has been taming grief for a long time. It therefore takes a lot of courage to allow our tears to flow, to risk expressing this emotion and perhaps to discover God's Spirit within it. There may be many Christians who struggle to pray as they were taught, feeling unfulfilled and guilty because God is not more real to them, without any awareness or encouragement that their embarrassing capacity for weeping at every opportunity is in fact the gift of the Spirit to them.

Shortly after the funeral of her father, a woman came to a Sunday service at St Stephen's church. She wept quietly throughout the service. She came the next week and the same happened again. It was some time before she was able to worship in church without tears. As the weeks went by it was clear that a new, deep and unexpected faith was being born in her. 'I know what was happening then,' she said, recalling the early weeks of tear-filled services. 'It was Jesus coming into my life.' Tears have continued to accompany her praying and worshipping. 'I don't feel sad,' she says. 'They come from deep inside me and I can't stop them.'

The language of tears

'Why are you weeping?' asked the angels. The question was not insensitive or mocking. Nor was Mary being criticised for a failure to rejoice in the resurrection. 'Christian mourning is a mourning of great delicacy,' writes Simon Tugwell, 'which does not despise or criticise or condemn'.[6]

Tears are a language. We must learn to question them and to listen to them. If we allow them, they lead us to the true source of our grief and our burden. Once we have come to that place and have recognised and named our pain, we can begin to move on. Anyone involved in the pastoral care of the bereaved or the traumatised knows the importance of the angel's question.

I remember once seeking out a pastoral friend to try and talk through a recurrent anxiety in my life. Barely into my story I found myself weeping helplessly. I ground to a halt, fumbling for my handkerchief and numbling ritual apologies for crying. My friend sat quietly with me, neither embarrassed nor concerned to calm me down. My tears were not an intrusion. They were the reason I had come. When the storm of emotion had stilled, my friend spoke quietly and gently: 'Tell me about your tears.' I realised in that moment that my tears had revealed more of my fears than my words would ever have allowed. Far from getting in the way, my tears were my guide to meeting my pain.

This needs discernment. Because of their fearful power and our vulnerability to tears, we try to control and misuse them. There may also be considerable confusion about guilt and responsibility in the cause of our grief. Tears can be merely sentimental. We can use them to manipulate sympathy and to influence situations for our own ends.

But when Jesus blesses those who mourn, he is blessing those who are willing to be truthful. They are people who mourn and lament life and death as they really are in this world. Their grief is 'the mourning of the realist, the penitent'.[7] And the Christian community is commanded to share in such grieving. St Paul didn't say 'cheer up those who weep': he said 'weep with them'. This is a very important insight. 'There can be no true rejoicing until we have stopped running away from mourning'.[8] Without a place for true grief and tears in Christian community, our search for joy and risen life with be dangerously superficial.

> Tears are always a sign that we are struggling with power of one sort or another: the loss of ours; the entering of God's. . . . The way and gift of tears opens the gate of death in this life to resurrection in this life. Tears release us from the prison of power and control into the vast love and infinite possibility of God.[9]

So it is only out of death that we find resurrection. It is only from tears that we enter joy.

Do not cling to me

It is probable that only those who have been through great tragedy can understand the desolation of Mary by the tomb. There comes a point in any bereavement when we can restrain ourselves no longer and our tears flow. For Mary the final breaking point is that even the body has vanished. Bitter despair, loss, hopelessness and utter confusion overwhelm her in a flood tide of grief.

But the story does not end in death. Someone is standing behind her. He questions her.

> Woman, why are you weeping? Whom are you looking for? The one you seek is in your possession, and you do not know it? You have the true, the eternal joy, and yet you weep? You stand outside, weeping at the tomb. Your heart is my tomb. And I am not dead there, but I take my rest in your heart, living for ever. Your soul is my garden. You were right to suppose that I was the gardener. I am the New Adam. I till and mind my paradise. Your tears, your love and your longing are all my work. In your inmost being you possess me, although you do not know it, and so you look for me without. Outwardly, therefore, I will appear to you, and so make you return to yourself, that in your inmost being you may find the one whom you seek outside.[10]

Now Jesus, the Second Adam, names his new creation: 'Mary.' She recognises Jesus for the first time and flings herself on him. But he will not let her: ' "Do not hold on to me, for I have not yet returned to the Father" ' (John 20:17).

It seems very harsh that in that moment of reunion Mary is so firmly pushed away. Yet she must let him go. There is a tough wisdom at work here. No relationship can survive when it is based on a fear of loss and death. For Cecil Day-Lewis, the bittersweet pain of this truth was summed up in the memory of watching his son walk away from him at the gates of school. He wrote of it in a moving poem called 'Walking Away'.

> I have had worse partings, but none that so
> Gnaws at my mind still. Perhaps it is roughly
> Saying what God alone could perfectly show –
> How selfhood begins with a walking away
> And love is proved in the letting go.[11]

There is a tendency to place a lot of emphasis on the first part of what Jesus said to Mary – 'Do not hold on to me.' The word here translated 'hold' also means 'cling'. While the Church spends a lot of time trying to draw 'outside' people into greater commitment to Christ, any Church leader knows the power of opposite temptation. Trying to help individuals to see that their devotion to Church activities has become possessive and clinging can be one of the most painful tasks of pastoral ministry. Whether it is running the flower rota, bell-ringing or indeed being the vicar, religious life can be peculiarly and fatally addictive. It is not just Mary who needs to hear this command of Jesus.

The actual reason Jesus gives for his insistence is often forgotten. 'Do not hold on to me, *for I have not yet returned to the Father.*' His mission is not yet complete. He has yet to ascend and take his throne. The Holy Spirit must be poured upon the Church. However tempting it might be for either of them, this is not the place to stop and rest.

Jesus still has work to do. And so does Mary: 'Do not hold on to me. Go instead to my brothers and tell them, "I am returning to my Father and your Father, to my God and your God".' (v. 17)

The end of tears

At the end of *Lord of the Rings*, the last terrible battle won against all the odds, Sam the Hobbit is overcome with joy at the celebrations. He had dreamed of this moment through the darkest struggles of the days before.

> He laughed aloud for sheer delight, and he stood up and cried: 'O great glory and splendour! And all my wishes have come true!' And then he wept. And all the host laughed and wept, and in the midst of their merriment and tears the clear voice of the minstrel rose like silver and gold, and all were hushed. And he sang to them, now in the Elven-tongue, now in the speech of the West, until their hearts, wounded with sweet words, overflowed, and their joy was like swords, and they passed in thought out to regions where pain and delight flow together, and tears are the very wine of blessedness.[12]

Resurrection life will always be inseparable from tears. For to receive the new life of Christ must also awaken, in us as in him, our grief for what still lies dead in this world. The resurrection community is a community of blessed mourners, longing for liberation but whose grief will not be comforted until all creation is restored in the gift of the risen Christ.

4 Stranger on the road
The walk to Emmaus

---

*Now that same day two of them were going to a village
called Emmaus, about seven miles from Jerusalem.
They were talking with each other about everything
that had happened. As they talked and discussed these
things with each other, Jesus himself came up and
walked along with them; but they were kept from
recognising him.*

*He asked them, 'What are you discussing together
as you walk along?'*

*They stood still, their faces downcast. One of them,
named Cleopas, asked him, 'Are you only a visitor
to Jerusalem and do not know the things that have
happened there in these days?'*

'What things?' he asked.

*'About Jesus of Nazareth,' they replied. 'He was a
prophet in word and deed before God and all the
people. The chief priests and our rulers handed him*

*over to be sentenced to death, and they crucified
him; but we had hoped that he was the one who was
going to redeem Israel. And what is more, it is the
third day since all this took place. In addition, some
of our women amazed us. They went to the tomb early
this morning but didn't find his body. They came and
told us that they had seen a vision of angels, who said
he was alive. Then some of our companions went to
the tomb and found it just as the women had said, but
him they did not see.'*   (Luke 24:13–24)

A pilgrim to the Holy Land today has a choice of four
possible sites for the village of Emmaus. All are roughly
the right distance from Jerusalem, but beyond that
nothing is certain. Nor does it matter: the significance
of this story is not the place they were going to, but
what happened on the way.

On the road going west from Jerusalem, a couple are
walking slowly and despondently among the pilgrims
leaving the city after the Passover festival. A stranger,
overhearing their conversation, asks them what they
are talking about. They stop on the road, and begin to
tell the stranger all that is burdening them. Luke
stresses their visible depression. Their story offers an
insight into the reaction of the disciples to the news
of the resurrection. Far from being good news, the
report of the empty tomb, the experience of the
women and the vision of angels had simply added to
the pain, turmoil and tragedy of that whole weekend.
Perhaps it was all too much for this couple. Before
Mary arrived with the astonishing story of her actual

meeting with the risen Jesus, they had decided to go home.

It is a surprising situation. We have a tendency to believe that the first disciples had an advantage over all later Christians because they were actually *there*. But this couple had followed Jesus, heard his teaching, seen his miracles, witnessed his death, and been told of his resurrection – and all without actually finding faith or spiritual understanding. For them it had ended in death, not life. Seeing is not necessarily believing.

The irony is that in the moment they decide to walk away from Jesus, Jesus appears to walk towards them. This paradox may be the clue to understanding the significance of the story.

Free gift

The story of the Emmaus road makes explicit what all the other resurrection encounters hint at. To recognise Jesus and to receive his new life is his gift alone. It is an awareness and understanding that cannot be arrived at by human reason alone. The helplessness and confusion of the disciples merely underline that.

The resurrection encounters are all the free acts of Jesus. This is in complete contrast to the events leading up to Easter, in which he had allowed himself to be 'handed over'. He became a powerless human being and 'gave himself up' into the hands of those who betrayed and crucified him. Now in his risen life Jesus is in control of every encounter. He comes and goes at his own will. His presence cannot be demanded. He is recognised only when he chooses to reveal himself. He is beholden to no one. The fate of those demoralised disciples depends entirely on the predisposition of Jesus towards them, as is made quite explicit in his words at the end of Matthew's gospel. On the mountain, Jesus claims the significance of his death and resurrection for the whole cosmic order: ' "All authority in heaven and on earth has been given to me' (Matt. 28:18).

What is unexpected on the Emmaus road is the sense of mischief that Jesus brings to this meeting. Firstly these disciples are deliberately prevented from recognising him. William Barclay's theory that the evening sun was dazzling them is clearly not what Luke had in mind: their blindness was due to an act of God, not to their eyes watering. Jesus joins them on the road, and plays the part of a friendly but ignorant stranger. He pretends he has been staying in that small city totally unaware that it was being rocked by religious and political crisis, culminating in the execution of a hugely popular spiritual leader. Even Cleopas is jolted out of his depression to ask him where he had been all weekend! And in drawing the story out of them, Jesus has the unusual experience of listening to his own obituary.

But the real encouragement of the story is that Jesus is there at all. He is deliberately seeking out two disciples who are walking away from it all.

There is a literary theory that all storytelling uses one of four plot types, which correspond to the four seasons of the year: tragedy corresponds to autumn, satire to winter, summer to romance. Applying this theory to St John's gospel, Mark Stibbe places the resurrection stories in the season of spring – the season of comedy. 'Comedy is inseparable from resurrection',[1] he writes. Luke has surely caught the same mood.

Holy play

This divine playfulness simply underlines human powerlessness and incomprehension in the presence of God's activity. It is not for us to grasp – it is for God to reveal. There is no easy way to accept where this leads us. It means there is an innate insecurity to the experience of following Jesus. He is beyond our command and control. We can do nothing about it. This is very hard to accept: Christian faith, after all, encourages us to believe that God is with us and committed to us. He forgives us and hears and answers our prayers. He loves to reveal his ways to us. All of this is gloriously true, but it leaves us perilously tempted to treat God as if he has placed himself at our command and only finds his purpose in his involvement in our lives. 'We are so preoccupied with God's relatedness, God being for us, that we do not attend enough to God's hiddenness', writes Walter Brueggemann.[2]

There is a necessary 'hiddenness' in God's dealings with us. It is partly for our own protection: we find it far too easy to take what is revealed and make it our final security. Our first encounter must be with our own blindness, and with the idols we have made of our own 'understanding' and 'certainties'. In order for the disciples to recognise the risen Jesus they had to first suffer the loss of what they thought they knew about

him. It may be that until that has happened Jesus is
not just unrecognised, but *unrecognisable*.

Jesus often taught that if we wanted to find life, we
must first be prepared to lose it. But we are probably
never prepared for how final that losing must be. This
story teaches us that there is a loss of faith and understanding that is necessary before we can recognise
Christ in his new life. There is no resurrection without
a dying first.

In Chapter 2 I referred to a time I spent in solitude
in the Alps. I had gone there to be alone. But the
experience was not what I expected; once exposed to
the stillness of the mountains I became insecure and
wanted God's presence. But

to my dismay the silence was empty. Even the most
familiar comforts of faith and assurance were missing.
It was a wilderness, and I had no way of knowing
how far it would stretch before me. I wept over God's
absence. I protested and got very angry. This was a
crisis of faith. How could I believe any more? Who was
God anyway? And I began to realise the nature of my
demands. The temptation to negotiate with God runs
so deep. I remembered Thomas Merton in his early
days as a monk, when all his longing for God seemed
only to meet a deep and disarming silence.

God is gift. He cannot be commanded. Up there in
that alpine cabin one morning, there came a tearful
and profound moment. Kneeling on the wooden floor
I told God I would no longer treat him as if I owned
him. Life was for him to give and for him to take away.
I confessed my attempts to control and dominate. I 'let

him go'. I asked for the life that was his gift alone.
Something died that day – and something was born.[3]

I hope I will not forget the shame of that encounter.
I came to see that in effect I had tried to organise a
retreat with God as if it were bookable, like a package
holiday. My plans were doomed to disaster. I
attempted to express the folly and confusion of my
attitude in a poem called 'Swissair hermit'.

> Here I am, God,
> scattered all over the Alps.
> No one reported the crash –
> rescuers will never find
> the pieces.
>
> I was on my way for a well-earned
> Package Solitude
>   (is this transmitting, God?),
> overloaded with thoughts and hopes,
> I couldn't make the height.
> Just folded in mid-air, I think,
>   (I'm trying to remember):
> lost all control, just
> broke up in mid-movie
> and fell to earth.
> No bomb suspected,
> none needed.
> Fatigue, maybe.
>
> Search for the wreckage, God,
>   (these silent peaks could hide the world) –
> find my black box.

Somewhere in the deepest gorge,
under pines and snow
battered, unconscious,
lying where it fell,
locked up with all
the mystery of who I was becoming
when it all began.

For more information on the crash, God,
the emergency number to ring is:
0181 (if you're outside London)
811 7915.
I'll repeat that,
0181 (if you're outside London)
811 7915.

Seen and unseen

Christian worship and prayer that celebrates only what
is 'seen' and 'revealed' is always in danger of being
shallow and superficial. The necessary corrective is
found in the Apophatic or 'Negative' theology taught
by the eastern Orthodox Church. 'Hidden' is actually a
better word for it – it is called 'Negative' in contrast to
'Positive' theology, which affirms and asserts what is
known and revealed about God. Apophatic theology
reminds us that in the end God cannot be known by
human understanding or reason. God is always beyond
our capacity to imagine him, picture him, understand
him, or put him into human language. The only way
is the way of agnosia, of *un*knowing.

The journey of faith towards God involves times

when there is a loss of words, understanding and vision of God. Although these are not wrong in themselves, they are limited and can easily mislead. The way of faith must include the gift of a darkness that exposes the emptiness of our concepts and ideas of God and of ourselves. It is a 'night of the senses', in which love and longing is all we have to offer. And these are all we need: 'Only loving can lead to the full knowledge that exceeds thought and words.'[4]

Kenneth Leech believes that the recovery of this teaching is vital for the Church in Western society today. In his manifesto for 'The New Dark Age' he stresses the need for a new reverence for the God who is hidden and dwells in mystery. Such a spirituality 'will seek to lead people away from a religion of easy answers into the dark night of faith. In an age of false certainties, of rigid fundamentalisms of various kinds, the renewal of mystical theology, the agnosia, the unknowing, is of the greatest importance'.[5]

He said to them, 'How foolish you are, and how slow to believe all that the prophets have spoken! Did not the Christ have to suffer these things and then enter into his glory?' And beginning with Moses and all the Prophets, he explained to them what was said in all the Scriptures concerning himself.   (Luke 24:25–7)

The way of unknowing, the loss of understanding, is not intended to be a way of ignorance. Christian mysticism is not mindless. On the Emmaus road Jesus hears the disciples' confession of confusion and roundly rebukes them for their unbelief and their lack of solid Bible study. 'Foolish' is a poor translation: he calls them 'dull' and 'slow', and the Greek here suggests that he speaks with strong emotion. Not for the first time Jesus is exasperated by disciples who cannot grasp what to him is apparently obvious.

But it is not the resurrection he teaches them about. It is the cross and his sufferings. Here Luke lets down his readers completely. He tells us that Jesus went through the entire Hebrew scriptures showing how they spoke of him, but for some reason omits to tell anyone what Jesus said! Christians ever since have been left with the frustrated feeling that this Bible study would have been the answer to a great many questions.

Yet the challenge of Jesus's rebuke can be levelled just as easily at today's Church: the Old Testament has long suffered from neglect, careless reading or misuse at the hands of the Christian community. The Church has rarely read and taught the Old Testament with the reverence, love and care that Jesus showed for it. 'Dull' would sum up the opinion of many who have encountered those scriptures in public worship. And when the text is not dull, often it is offensive and harsh to modern ears. The use of the Old Testament tends to be highly selective: an unacknowledged censorship operates around the more awkward and difficult passages, in much the same way that brackets are coyly printed around parts of the psalms, inviting us to omit sentiments we might find offensive.[6]

For that reason, I wonder whether the stress in Jesus' rebuke was on the word *all*: 'all that the prophets have spoken'. To find the suffering and crucified God foreshadowed in 'all' the Old Testament requires a willingness to wrestle with the darker and more painful corners of what is written there. Even the disciples hadn't done that until they were forced to.

From my own experience of preaching and leading study groups there remains a basic problem with the Old Testament for many people today. The fact is that the world and the words of the Old Testament feel strange and very alien to modern ears. It is also popularly believed that radical Biblical criticism has fatally undermined the credibility and reliability of the Old Testament.

For many, these scriptures are no longer actively believed and believable in the way that Jesus called the disciples to believe in them. In such circumstances it is easier to dip into favourite passages, stories and psalms, rather than to struggle to try and see the story as a whole. But while our knowledge of these scriptures revolves only around the safety and warmth of God's promises and blessings, the faith that results will be dull and slow of heart, and Christ will remain a stranger.

Living proof

In more conservative Christian traditions, the Old Testament tends to be mined at this point as a resource for verses, teachings and 'proof texts' that appear to point to Christ. 'The Old Testament contains over 300 references to the Messiah that were fulfilled by Jesus', declares Josh McDowell.[7] Such study is clearly encouraged by Jesus himself, but we should beware of declaring too certainly what the Bible chooses not to state directly. The Bible is not to be treated like a spiritual equivalent of a car maintenance manual. The Christian understanding of revelation is not finally of a written text, but of a living God.

Jesus insisted that their knowledge and trust in the Bible was inadequate. But we have no good reason for believing that he quoted three hundred Old Testament proof texts at the disciples. Nor did they need a study on the doctrine of the inspiration of the Bible. There are times when this approach to belief comes very close to a 'salvation by words'.

G. B. Caird suggests that it is a mistake to look for predictions and statements as such.

> We look in vain for Old Testament predictions that the Messiah must reach his appointed glory through suffering, unless we realise that the Old Testament is concerned from start to finish with the call and destiny of Israel, and that the Messiah, as King of Israel, must embody in his own person the character and vocation of his own people.[8]

Through the scriptures Jesus led them to recognise the character of God in the midst of his world, finally and fully revealed in the sufferings of Christ.

Rowan Williams' comment is helpful here. He points out that in the Bible there is a meeting of God's world and ours. We must recognise our own place in the stories that are written there. Asking how we respond to the times when part of the Bible seems obscure, harsh or just impossible to understand, he writes:

> Must we not say something like the following? Scripture we know is not simply an oracle. It is not simply lapidary remarks dropped down from heaven and written on stone. . . . we may be more helped by reflecting on the story of Jacob wrestling with the angel than by any images of oracles from heaven. Here in scripture is God's urgency to communicate, here in scripture is our mishearing, our misappropriating, our deafness and our resistance. Woven together in scripture are those two things, the giving of God and our inability to receive what God wants to give. On almost every page of the gospels we read: 'Jesus said, "Do you understand?" They said, "No." '
>
> We read with a sense of our own benighted savagery in receiving God's gift, and our solidarity with those writers of scripture caught up in the blazing fire of God's gift who yet struggle with it, misapprehend it, and misread it.'[9]

As they approached the village to which they were going, Jesus acted as if he were going further. But they urged him strongly, 'Stay with us, for it is nearly evening; the day is almost over.' So he went in to stay with them.

When he was at table with them, he took bread, gave thanks, broke it and began to give it to them. Then their eyes were opened and they recognised him, and he disappeared from their sight. They asked each

*other, 'Were not our hearts burning within us while
he talked with us on the road and opened the Scriptures to us?'*

They got up and returned at once to Jerusalem.

(Luke 24:28–33)

When they reach Emmaus, Jesus makes as if to continue his journey. This may be more mischief on his
part, for he has yet to complete his ministry to this
couple. But we may also recognise the courtesy of
Christ. He does not force himself upon them. He does
not presume his invitation into their home. For the
first time he waits for them to take the initiative. His
presence has captivated them, however, and they 'urge'
him to stay.

At the meal table the moment comes for his revealing to them. He has carefully prepared them for this
moment. He has walked with them, unseen. He has
taught them from the scriptures, and ministered to
them by the gift of his Spirit burning within them as
they walked. In a moment of moving intensity at the
evening meal, he takes bread, blesses it and breaks it
for them.

It is very significant that this should be the moment
for their eyes to open. The risen Jesus is to be recognised as the same Jesus of the last supper. He is the
suffering and crucified one, who has now entered into
glory.

Open eyes

In the moment of recognition he vanishes, but there is no despondency at this. At the beginning of the story his loss had left them desolate. Now it leaves them fulfilled. His ministry to them is complete. The rumour is confirmed: what was lost has now been found. His final gift to them is their recognition of *themselves* in all that has happened: 'Did not our hearts burn within us?' Their real journey can now begin.

For Gregory of Nyssa, a teacher firmly in the 'Hidden' tradition of theology, this losing and finding are one and the same thing in our encounter with God. It cannot be otherwise:

> to find God is to seek him unceasingly. Here to seek is not one thing and to find another. The reward of the search is to go on searching. The soul's desire is fulfilled by the very fact of remaining unsatisfied, for really to see God is never to have had one's fill of desiring him.'[10]

The Emmaus Road story has sustained the paradox of losing and finding, blindness and sight, to its very close.

5 Some of our women amazed us
Women, men and the subversiveness of resurrection

'. . . some of our women amazed us. They went to the tomb early this morning but didn't find his body. They came and told us that they had seen a vision of angels, who said he was alive. . . .' (Luke 24:22–3)

When Jesus rose early on the first day of the week, he appeared first to Mary Magdalene . . . She went and told those who had been with him . . . When they heard that Jesus was alive and that she had seen him, they did not believe it. (Mark 16:9–11)

You don't believe me.

YOU DON'T BELIEVE ME!

I tell you I saw him. It was our Lord.

The men are silent. She makes to leave.

Women's fantasies *says a voice from the back.*

She turns back in anger.

Fantasy! Was his death a fantasy? I saw him die, I wept at his feet.

Why should he not appear to me?

He is risen.

The men are still silent and expressionless.

She gives up, utterly frustrated, and turns to leave.

He told me to tell you

(*she shrugs*) – and I have done so.

She leaves, slamming the door.[1]

The scene is from Franco Zeffirelli's film, *Jesus of Nazareth*. Mary Magdalene has come straight from the tomb to the disciples. She is so transfigured in the telling of her meeting with Jesus that it takes her a while to realise that they are staring at her with blank disbelief. She looks at them with astonishment and then her frustration boils over. The disciples had a double shock to cope with on that first Easter day. Jesus had risen from the dead. And the first person he had chosen to tell was a woman.

The news of the resurrection broke upon the world as a rumour spread by women. Anyone wanting to claim that these stories were made up by later Christians has to explain the scandal of this central detail. In the culture of those days, no one inventing a resurrection story would start like this. And no one would be expected to believe it.

But if the word of Mary is true, God has done the unthinkable. He has cut right across all social and religious traditions of that time. In a world in which all authority is vested in men, God has given his greatest revelation to a woman. In a society in which the testimony of a woman is not even accepted in a court of law, Jesus has made a woman his apostle ('sent one') to the men. She deserves a unique honour. She became 'for some hours the confessing church on earth'.[2] God is being very subversive.

It is entirely predictable that such a witness should be dismissed out of hand by the men, at least initially: 'their words seemed to them like nonsense' (Luke 24:11). If God wanted to say something important, they must have thought, he said it to men. Later that day, however, Cleopas admits to the stranger on the Emmaus road that the story had amazed them enough to check it: 'some of our companions went to the tomb and found it just as the women had said' (Luke 24:24). But when the disciples meet in Jerusalem to confirm the discovery that Jesus had risen, it is not the women's witness that is celebrated – their word is still without honour. ' "It is true! The Lord has risen and has appeared to *Simon*" ' (Luke 24:34; my italics).

The same thing happens when St Paul writes to the Corinthian Church about the death and resurrection of Christ. He lists all the appearances of Jesus to the male disciples, includes himself ('last of all'), but completely omits Mary and any of the women (1 Cor. 15:5–8).

Silent witnesses

It is very clear from the gospel accounts that Jesus was revolutionary in his friendship, openness and acceptance of women. It is less often noted how alive and liberated women were in relating to him. In St John's gospel alone women have a central part in nearly half the most significant scenes. Martha and Mary, Mary Magdalene, the woman at the well – all related to Jesus with a directness and a vitality that was not evident among many of the men. The women were also faithful to Jesus, staying with him through his suffering and crucifixion while all but John among the men had deserted.

But the gospels themselves are almost totally the testimony and theology of men, in fact they hardly record the words of women at all. So if we ask, 'How did the female disciples experience following Jesus and understanding his teaching?', the answer is 'We do not know.' They are never allowed to tell the story in their own words.

Until I saw the resurrection scene in Zeffirelli's film it had not occurred to me to wonder how Mary reacted to being disbelieved: the gospel does not tell us. The anger and authority with which she rebuked the other disciples came as a shock. So there is always a gap, a silence, in the witness of the first Christian community. The story has only been heard from one side. We are left wondering.

Another example of this is the story of the appearance of Jesus to two disciples on the road to Emmaus, mentioned above and discussed more fully in the previous chapter. There has long been a curiosity about who the disciples were. Luke names one of them, Cleopas, in a way that suggests they would *both* have been known to his readers. Cleopas also appears in John's gospel as the husband of Mary, one of the women who stood by the cross.

But who was the other disciple? Throughout the story the other disciple is 'spoken for' in a way that culturally suggests a woman, and a woman would not be expected to speak to another man in public. Cleopas would not have been travelling with a woman other than his wife. Had the other disciple been a man he would surely have been named, whereas in the gospels women are generally only named in their own right when no men are present. Finally, when they arrive at Emmaus the stranger is invited into *their* home ('Stay with *us*', Luke 24:29).

On these grounds it has long been thought likely that the other disciple was in fact Mary, Cleopas' wife. This was an important family in the early Church. Their son Simeon became one of the first Bishops of Jerusalem. The telling of this story would have had added significance to first generations of the new Church.

This inference means also that this silent listener on the road was one of the women at the cross. It is highly likely that she knew a great deal about the events at the tomb that morning – perhaps she was there. Certainly the women would have talked together.

Of course we don't actually know. We are making connections. Trying to honour the witness of women in the New Testament has always had to involve some detective work and reconstruction, and I am not pretending otherwise. But there is a certain irony in picturing a depressed Cleopas relating secondhand stories about Jesus, to Jesus, in front of his wife who just might have known it all firsthand anyway!

A different story

Whatever the faltering intentions of the first Christian community, for the greater part of the long history of the Church, this one-sided witness became institutionalised. With a few exceptions, leadership, theology and worship have been solidly and jealously the work of men in the Church. Only now are we beginning to hear another side to the same story.

A theological college lecturer has written of her growing pain while training people for ministry within such an implacably male tradition:

> A feeling somehow grew that, in the texts of theology, my women students and I did not exist. Something important about us and our lives had not gone into forming this rich doctrinal, liturgical and pastoral mixture . . . somehow women's voices had not been heard, and we were all the losers for it.
>
> I remember thinking on one particularly grim day, 'It doesn't matter, because God loves women!' – and somehow, and to my surprise, this recognition made me weep with relief. Of course, I had never consciously doubted that God loved women. But somehow the barrage of ancient opinion, the structures into which

one was perceived to fit oddly, the little niggling ...
negativities which one felt in a place which fit the
young male candidates like a glove, all conspired to
make one feel that women were not really quite as
good as men, that God didn't care about women *quite*
as much as men, that women's sufferings (so many of
them not even figuring on the ethics or pastoral
courses) did not matter *quite* as much as those of men,
that what happened to women in the home didn't
matter *quite* as much as what happened to men in
the work-place. In short, that somehow women didn't
figure except as sources of gynaecological problems in
Christian ethics, or people to make tea.[3]

The painful irony of a Church that has left women
feeling left out is that it has never solved the problem
of the men absent from its congregations.

A Religious sister offers a telling insight into this
situation from her experience of leading prayer and
meditation groups. She encourages the members to
imagine themselves at the cross. They are asked to picture the scene, the sounds, the light, the smells, the
atmosphere. Then they watch the dying Christ, his
struggles to breathe. . . . 'Now,' she says, 'you are there,
what do you do?'

And the extraordinary thing is, that, almost without
exception, men can't take it. They go away. They simply
can't stand to watch that intensity of suffering. So they
slope off. Women can't stand it either. But they are
determined to save him. So they fling themselves at
the cross to cut him free. Or they start rallying the
crowds to take on the Roman soldiers. The one thing

they can't manage in the face of such evident wretched-
ness, is inactivity.[4]

In his fascinating book, *The Intimate Connection*,[5]
James Nelson observes that this tendency to walk away
from emotionally difficult situations is a painful mark
of the male in our culture. He disembodies himself
from physical reality. He cuts out and finds himself
unable to relate. The search for absent fathers demon-
strates just one feature of that. Nelson suggests that a
primary task for men in our society is to recover an
awareness and acceptance of their own bodily existence. Significantly he writes that the male recovery of
the body will lead to a 'recovery of resurrection faith'.
Resurrection faith is always a resurrection of the body.

The word of a woman

The New Testament writings themselves reflect the
tension and confusion of a Church trying to live faith-
fully with a new vision for the partnership of women
and men. The word and example Jesus left them with
was disturbingly radical and far-reaching. So much so
that Archbishop George Carey has suggested that the
first Christians could not have seen the implications of
their own teachings.[6]

Old ways of thinking keep resurfacing. Soon after
greeting men and women as co-leaders in his Churches,
and despite declaring that in Christ there is 'neither
Jew nor Greek, male nor female', St Paul goes on calling
his readers 'brothers' and encouraging them as *'Sons
of God'*. That his writing and sermon illustrations

appear to be almost exclusively drawn from the world
of men – wrestling, boxing, athletics, for example –
further highlights the problem. Old habits die hard,
even in the resurrection life.

We don't know, for example, whether anyone suggested that Mary Magdalene might be on the shortlist
to replace Judas among the apostles. She had everything on the job description but the right sex. Perhaps
it was argued 'the time was not right'.

At the end of the letter to the Romans, however, in
a long list of warm greetings to women and men in the
church there, we find St Paul personally greeting 'And-
ronicus and *Junias*' (a woman), telling us they have
been in prison with him for the faith and that 'they are
outstanding among the *apostles*'. He names a woman
among the apostles.[7]

It is clear that women ministered, prophesied, taught
and took authority alongside men in the resurrection
Church. In first-century Hebrew and Greek cultures
such a partnership must have needed courage and a
wise flexibility. There was always the risk of confusion
and misunderstanding.

While it is also true that there are teachings that
apparently contradict each other over the place and
ministry of women in the Church, a belated awareness
has been growing that the Church has been applying
these teachings without a full understanding of the
original context in which they were written.[8]

Breaking silence

This is not an abstract discussion. The social consequences of this dualism have been devastating down the centuries and continue to cause suffering across the world today. 'To be born of a woman is plain fact,' wrote Alan Ecclestone, 'to be born a woman has been for the most part a misfortune'.[9]

Even now, after years of campaigning, the average wages for women in Britain remain significantly lower than for men, while the demands of home and child care remain almost as great as ever. In the event of the breakdown of marriage, it is women who are the parents in the majority of one-parent families. Recent research has shown that 60 per cent of such families are living at below half the national average income. In times of economic recession it is women who bear the brunt of the sacrifices. Women wanting to pursue a career are still expected to juggle work and family responsibilities at the same time:

> For decades, feminists have been thinking imaginatively about the dual roles that women play. It is men who are the problem. It is time for fathers to break the silence on their own twin tasks, to work more flexibly, even at financial cost to themselves. The state and employers should support a culture in which men (and women) do not have to sacrifice children for career.[10]

New man, new woman

In such a society, the Church that began with the calling of a woman on resurrection day still has far to go in honouring the partnership it is called to. The stories of women in the faith are still neglected, excluded or used very selectively in the Christian community. The Christian Calendar used by the Church of England honours the lives of 85 holy men, but can find only 11 women to include. The more extensive Roman Catholic list reveals the same proportionate bias. It is clear that in the process of recognising sanctity, sexual politics is at least as influential as holy living.

In the cycle of daily scripture readings chosen for public worship, many of the most glorious and positive stories of women's faith and obedience seem to be missing. This means that regular worshippers at traditional Anglican worship have simply not been hearing the word and witness of faithful women alongside those of men from the Bible. By contrast most of the stories of 'fallen' and 'sinful' women are included.

Take the moving story of the woman anointing Jesus with expensive perfume. All four gospels record it. But only Luke mentions that she is a known sinner in that community and stresses her need for forgiveness (Luke 7:36ff). Mark and Matthew record the other side of that story – that her anointing of Jesus was a powerful prophetic ministry to Jesus and that he gloriously affirmed her: 'She has done a beautiful thing . . . wherever the gospel is preached throughout the world, what she has done will also be told, in memory of her' (Mark 14:6, 9).

Well, except in the Church of England, that is. Luke's story of the forgiven prostitute is chosen as a eucharistic reading on the tenth Sunday after Pentecost. Mark's account, to be told 'wherever the gospel is preached' is set for reading on a Tuesday morning, the week after the 3rd Sunday in Epiphany. A Church that only reads aloud stories of *fallen* and *sinful* women is not likely to find the suggestion of women in leadership very compelling.

The lack of women's experience impoverishes much of our liturgy, as well. This is never more evident than in the liturgy of baptism. When Jesus wants to describe how God brings us to new life he speaks of the wonder and vulnerability of a baby being born out of its mother's womb. We are born out of the womb of God's love (John 3:3). But in the Anglican baptism service the water is blessed with the more impersonal symbols of washing dirt away, of the Red Sea parting, and of the dark waters of death. The picture most precious to the experience of Jesus, and most fundamental to our experience – childbirth – is excluded.[11]

Healing the split

When Jesus asks the Church to hear the news of resurrection from the lips of a woman he is asking us to listen very carefully. In a society where women were always followers, he chose a woman to lead. In a culture that required women to be silent, Jesus gave them a message to proclaim. In a world where women were treated as second class, he rose to greet them first.

It is evident that the Christian Church for most of its history has been unable to recognise the implications of the example of Jesus in this resurrection sign. Although the message of Easter was heard through the voice of a woman, women's voices and ministry have more often been refused in the mission of the gospel.

Whether men have been any more fulfilled in their persistent denial of genuine partnership with women in the ministry of the gospel is an open question. There is surely a price to be paid for trying to carry the whole story of humanity alone. 'That is the fault of so much male-written theology over the centuries,' writes James Nelson. 'It assumed it was speaking universally, when in fact it was speaking out of a particular male experience'.[12] The recovery of the partnership of men and women does not offer only women the possibility of new recognition and fulfilment: men too will encounter themselves in a new light.

As I watched the first women being ordained priest in the Church of England, I felt an unexpected sense of relief: a relief that at last a burden was being shared, as had always been intended. No longer were men the self-appointed managers of the world and the sole mediators of God within it – we never were, anyway; we had not listened to the Easter gospel. But now we can rest a little. We can even be led.

But we should not be surprised that this particular journey to risen life is so long and painful. The Bible is clear that the division between men and women is second only to the division between God and his world. Monica Furlong suggests that the day that a pregnant woman presides as priest at the Eucharist will be the beginning of healing for the deepest split in the Christian Church – not just the split between male and female, but the division between spirituality and sexuality.[13] God is not overturning one hierarchy to replace it with another. He is calling women and men to a new relationship.

If this is the place to which the Church of England has now come, no one can accuse it of hurrying. It was highly appropriate that, rather than ordaining women priests on the traditional feast days of the very male and hierarchical St Peter or the great Archangel Michael, the Diocese of London held its services on the same weekend as the London Marathon!

I hope they said sorry

I hope they said sorry, those male disciples. I need to say sorry too, somehow, somewhere.

It needs saying. Sorry that we have been so slow to believe. Sorry for not naming those we journeyed with. Sorry that whole dimensions of human experience have been excluded from worship and prayer; that so much of the masculine inheritance in the faith has been the privileged fruit of deep, sustained injustice, a wilful rejection, unbelief and a need to control. Sorry for the refusal to believe the word of a woman on that Easter morning. I repent of my sins.

It is only right that I close with a confession: I must declare a personal interest. This chapter began life as a sermon I preached at my wife Jackie's first Eucharist, the day after her ordination as priest in the Church of England. She was, at the time, eight months pregnant.

It felt like resurrection. For at last it is women – in direct line with Mary at the empty tomb that first Easter morning – women who proclaim the death and resurrection of Christ in the breaking of the bread.

'It is true! The Lord has risen and has appeared to *Mary.*'

6 It's flesh I'm talking about here!

The resurrection of the body

While they were still talking about this, Jesus himself stood among them and said to them, 'Peace be with you.' They were startled and frightened, thinking they saw a ghost. He said to them, 'Why are you troubled, and why do doubts rise in your minds? Look at my hands and my feet. It is I myself! Touch me and see; a ghost does not have flesh and bones, as you see I have.' . . .

'Do you have anything here to eat?' They gave him a piece of broiled fish, and he took it and ate it in their presence. (Luke 24:36–9, 41–3)

In James Morrow's novel *Towing Jehovah*,[1] God has died of unknown causes and his body has fallen from heaven into the Atlantic Ocean, just south of the Equator. The archangels want him to have a proper burial. The Vatican realises the need for secrecy. A huge supertanker is chartered to find the body and tow it to a remote tomb under the North Pole. On board, a motley crew of sailors, theologians, atheists and feminists alike struggle to absorb the implications. God had a *body* after all. God was *male* after all. He *existed* after all. God has *died.*

The whole black comedy unfolds as the divine corpse, over two miles long, is slowly towed by its ears towards the Arctic.

Out of the body

The traditional belief that Jesus rose from death with a physical body is a subject of much debate in today's Church. On one level this is hardly surprising, for the Church has never been sure what to make of *anyone*'s body, particularly. A perverse and destructive dualism between 'spirit' and 'matter' has infected so much of the understanding of the Church that we have been left with little positive use for the body at all. It has often been treated as a burden, to be towed around in this mortal life while the 'spirit' within longs for its freedom. 'The flesh' has always been an embarassment or an enemy. The phrase itself instantly conjures up something forbidden and illicit; for the faithful, life in the body is to be endured rather than celebrated. The really important parts of the Christian life are the 'spiritual' parts, such as worship and prayer. Our bodies have to come along as well, of course; but like resentful children, dragged by the ears and knowing instinctively where they are not really welcome, they get bored, fidget, and cause a distraction. The body is a temporal nuisance.

Of course it is never spelled out so crudely, but we learn this split in all sorts of ways. At Sunday school I learned that in order to pray and to be with God, the body had to be kept still – 'hands together, eyes closed'. I learned that if I turned my 'eyes upon Jesus the things of earth would grow dim'.[2] In church services I learned that our bodies were largely irrelevant to the real purpose of being there. They were left to suffer the hardship of the old wooden pews, Victorian heating systems and kneelers filled with concrete.

On certain embarassing evenings at Christian youth camps I was told that my body was full of awkward and powerful passions (a discovery I had already made). The speaker was often too embarassed to speak very freely, but I learned that these were wonderful but wrong and needed strictly controlling in case I enjoyed them. Though no one ever claimed that marriage was a remedy against lust (as the old Prayer Book said), there was an adult anxiety running through all these talks which would clearly only be relieved when we were all 'safely' married. In confirmation classes I learned that my body was the 'Temple of the Holy Spirit' – which never sounded very exciting, in all honesty, and which seemed to be all about behaviour and little to do with pleasure. 'Life in the Spirit', at that stage, had all the attraction of disinfectant.

It is not surprising that in such a Church we pray with eyes shut, for 'spiritual life' requires becoming *less* aware of the things of earth. 'Holiness is tantamount to bodilessness and saints are sexless people, mystically

attuned to a life transcending earthly matter.'[3] No, not
sex*less* so much as sex-*denying*. Why else do we find
the word 'virgin' alongside the names of holy women
in the Church calendar of Saints, as if no other detail
of their lives is needed to explain their sanctity? Saint
equals no sex; holiness equals no body.

Is it really surprising that a Church that has been
embarrassed for so long by its own fleshly reality could
come eventually to resist the idea of the flesh of God?

Written on the body

The Christian faith is incurably and unavoidably physical. William Temple described it as the most material-
istic of all religions: it is faith in a God who has taken
flesh and made his home in our physical, earthy nature.
So Christian faith can never be about the liberating of
our 'spirit' out of 'flesh'. It is about the hope of the
union and transformation of spirit *and* matter, made
one and whole in the love of Christ. Such a faith should
change the way we relate to our own bodies. It is holy
stuff, this flesh and blood: God has taken it as his own.

The gospel stories clearly emphasise the physical
reality of the risen Jesus, indeed they go out of their
way to stress this. In fact popular Jewish belief at that
time would not have assumed that resurrection was
anything other than bodily. To be sure it was a body
with new 'agilities'.[4] Jesus could appear and disappear
at will. He was very difficult to recognise until he chose
to reveal himself, and he could overhear conversations
at which he was not physically present.

But in front of the startled and frightened disciples

Jesus went out of his way to assure them that it was really him ('It is I', Luke 24:39) and to demonstrate to them the solidity and reality of his physical nature ('Do you have anything here to eat?'). The disciples at Emmaus never questioned that they had travelled with a real human being. Mary in the garden, even out of traumatic grief, never doubted she was talking to a real person. We note rather that she clung to him physically and had to be asked to let go. Finally Thomas was invited to physically touch Jesus' wounds.

All of which, however startling and hard to believe, is completely consistent with the story that has gone before. God has always been involved in physical things. He lived, suffered and died in our flesh. And now he rises from death and is glorified in our flesh.

We have to remain reverently agnostic about what the texts do not attempt to tell us. The risen Jesus is not physically described at all. We don't know what he looked like. The curiosity is natural. He had left his grave-clothes, for example, so was he naked when he appeared to the disciples? The thought was a little too much for St Bernard, who had to reassure anxious readers that in the event 'the eye of love clothes the vision in familiar garments'![5]

What is plain from all the accounts is that disciples were left in no doubt that they were meeting a physical human being. Someone who can pass through walls, appearing and disappearing, is normally assumed to be *less* substantial – ghost or apparition. C. S. Lewis suggested that the 'agility' of the risen Jesus reveals that the life he has entered in our flesh is actually *more* real and solid than ours, not less.[6]

The ancient Easter liturgies of the Church have always celebrated the resurrection with very physical and sensual imagery. They use the language of marriage and the wedding night. The Easter tomb is our tomb. Christ comes to the tomb as a bridegroom. He comes to the death of our earthly nature and brings it to life. The tomb becomes a bedroom. So the resurrection has been described as 'the consummation of the marriage of heaven and earth'.[7]

That God has this quite improbable love affair with our physical nature is beyond our imagining. But he clearly does. As Rubem Alves puts it,

> God's desire is revealed in our bodies. After all, what the doctrine of the incarnation whispers to us is that God, eternally, wants a body like ours. Have you ever thought about this . . . our body, as something that God desires?[8]

And what do *we* think about it? How would we feel standing naked in front of a mirror, or lying in the bath, reading those words aloud.

God wants a body like mine! 'Jesu, lover of my . . . *body*' – how does that sound?

Body positive

That the hope of resurrection should include our physical bodies is a liberating thought. We live in a culture that forces upon us impossible expectations and our bodies carry the burden of them. The powerful multinational advertising industry deliberately exploits our physical unease. It constantly parades before us models of impossible physical perfection. And the subtext is clear: even after you've bought the right floor polish, drunk the right coffee, driven the right car, and worn the right clothes, you still haven't got the body you need – and deep down you know it.

The body in our culture is exploited ruthlessly. It absorbs all the burdens of our emotional and spiritual dis-ease. And in our despair we make impossible demands upon it to present us to the world with the images we think we need. 'In the factory I make products,' said Charles Revlon, 'in the market place I create dreams.'

Rubem Alves suggests that the exploitation of the body is one of the consequences of a loss of belief in the incarnation. 'For if God is found beyond the body, anything can be done to the body'.[9] So to find God physically at home in the very part of our nature that leaves us alienated and abused is itself a gift to a world like ours. It is the ground of our hope, for our existence is incurably and inescapably physical.

Body shop

In contrast to the diffidence of Christian theology, our society has been showing a new attentiveness and sensitivity towards the body in recent years. There is an awareness that it is part of the whole person and should be treated with love and respect.

Health and fitness centres have appeared everywhere. Alternative health remedies have stressed the healing power of physical touch (as in massage), and the use of the senses to reduce stress (as in aromatherapy). Lifestyle and diet have become more important. Body-positive therapies have claimed much success in treating serious illness through helping people discover a more healthy relationship with their physical bodies. This has been especially important where viruses such as HIV have left sufferers facing actual rejection within their bodies.

Hand in hand with this has gone the explosion of spiritual hunger and curiosity, and a growing interest in meditation systems, transcendental meditation, yoga, religious cults, Eastern philosophies, the New Age, and encounter and self-realisation programmes.

All this has spawned an enormous and lucrative 'health awareness' industry that can become another form of bodily exploitation. This enthusiasm easily becomes obsessional and must therefore be approached with care and discernment. But what we must recognise is the hunger behind all this: it is a longing to live whole in a world which has divided us up.

Beginning as some-body

Where the body and the spirit are recognised together in relating to God, there is new life. There is resurrection. It brings a quite new vitality. That is why I believe in the resurrection of the body.

For many this has to begin with a willingness to recognise our own bodies and to 'own' them for the first time. Many people feel very ill at ease with their bodies, and in effect ignore them. When leading prayer groups or retreats I sometimes suggest that individuals go to their rooms and explore the experience of praying to God naked. The idea is always greeted with nervous laughter. And people are always surprised by how much courage it actually takes to do it.

One person wrote to me about the experience.

I locked the door and drew the curtains and lay naked on my bed. It felt very very strange. I contemplated each part of my body. I tried to be aware of how I felt about it. All sorts of feelings surfaced as I did so. There were tears and there was laughter. Bit by bit I offered myself, bodily, to God – *for the first time* [my italics]. It still felt very strange. Over the next few weeks I kept praying that way until the strangeness passed. It was a profound and very important thing to have done.

Another participant spoke movingly of how the experience had not only released him into a new awareness of God's love, it had also brought him newfound sexual freedom in his marriage. We should not be surprised. In the affirming of our bodies as good, our deepest needs are ministered to and released. Christian spirituality is marked by a journey *towards* the flesh. It requires that we become more physical, not less. We are followers of Jesus – in his incarnation and resurrection.

Christian teaching on prayer and meditation these days has found a much more positive place for the body. This is long overdue. For so long, Christian worship has asked us to be no-bodies. The word is very revealing. To be a no-body in our society is to be unrecognised as a real person. We relate as bodies. And what Jesus affirms is that when we come to God we don't come to God as *no*-bodies, or *any*-bodies. We come as *some*-bodies. He calls us by name.

There has also been a greater confidence to allow our senses to be part of our awareness of life and God. We are allowed to pray with eyes open, taking in the created world. We can taste, and watch, and smell, and listen. We are learning to risk being fully alive before God.

If our praying has always been inhibited by the need for special language and phrases, the discovery that we can pray through our bodies – expressing our prayers through simple actions rather than words – may be wonderfully liberating.

Reunion

Whenever spiritual renewal or revival has come to the Church in its history, it has been marked by a reviving of the body. At times the result may be startlingly dramatic. The so-called 'Toronto blessing' is the most recent example of this. The physical and emotional behaviour at such meetings is unusual, often startling, and needs wise pastoral handling. The movement has its critics. But another extreme has long been more evident in the Church. It is rarely acknowledged what rigid controls on the emotions and the body have been required to attend traditional Church of England services.

In her wonderful study of Mary Magdalene, *Transformed by Love*, Sister Margaret Magdalene suggests that the strong controls which mark out the expression of much traditional worship can disguise, in part, a fear of passion. She observes how regularly through history the Church has pushed the emotions and passion of believing to the edge of its life. In the name of decency and order we have kept the passion of believing under wraps.

> We have dammed up our tears, stifled our spontaneity and curbed the Charismatics. We have applied reason and even cynicism to the 'unusual' – the miraculous healings, the spontaneous outbursts of song, the welling up of the heart and the desire to share the resulting joy. We have applied restraint within ourselves and upon others. We have tried to confine boundless joy and reduce it to manageable proportions.
>
> We have, quite simply, quenched the Spirit by allowing ourselves to become prisoners to our own fear.[10]

Love it, love it hard

The novelist Toni Morrison has often written of the importance of the body to peoples struggling to discover their own life and destiny out of oppression. 'Love your body' is a strong theological theme in her writing in a way that always combines protest and celebration (as perhaps the resurrection does too). In *Beloved*, Baby Suggs preaches to her slave congregation:

> In the silence that followed, Baby Suggs, holy, offered up to them her great big heart.
>
> She did not tell them to clean up their lives or to go and sin no more. She did not tell them they were

the blessed of the earth, its inheriting meek or its glorybound pure.

She told them that the only grace they could have was the grace they could imagine. That if they could not see it, they would not have it.

'Here,' she said, 'in this place, we flesh; flesh that weeps, laughs; flesh that dances on bare feet in grass. Love it. Love it hard. Yonder they do not love your flesh. They despise it. They don't love your eyes; they's just as soon pick em out. No more do they love the skin on your back. Yonder they flay it. And O my people they do not love your hands. Those they only use, tie, bind, chop off and leave empty. Love your hands! Love them. Raise them up and kiss them. Touch others with them, pat them together, stroke them on your face 'cause they don't love that either. *You* got to love it, *you*! And no, they ain't in love with your mouth. Yonder out there, they will see it broken and break it again. What you say out of it they will not heed. What you scream from it they do not hear. What you put into it to nourish your body they will snatch away and give you leavins instead. No, they don't love your mouth. *You* got to love it. This is flesh I'm talking about here. Flesh that needs to be loved. Feet that need to rest and dance; backs that need support; shoulders that need arms, strong arms I'm telling you. And O my people, out yonder, hear me, they do not love your neck unnoosed and straight. So love your neck; put a hand on it, grace it, stroke it and hold it up.'[11]

Postscript

After I finished writing this chapter I began to save it on the computer. Each chapter is stored under one word from its title. My computer showed a rare flash of human intuition. On the screen it asked this question:

'Save flesh before closing?'   Yes/No

Of course. That's what this chapter is all about.

7   The wounds that keep us
The risen presence of Jesus

On the evening of that first day of the week, when the disciples were together, with the doors locked for fear of the Jews, Jesus came and stood among them and said, 'Peace be with you!' After he said this, he showed them his hands and side. The disciples were overjoyed when they saw the Lord.

Again Jesus said, 'Peace be with you! As the Father has sent me, I am sending you.' And with that he breathed on them and said, 'Receive the Holy Spirit.'

(John 20:19–22)

Something strange is going on when a crowd of people start celebrating at the sight of a scarred and wounded body. When did the sight of someone disfigured or tortured last fill you with joy?

Something strange is going on when it is a glorified

but *wounded* man who stands before us on the day of resurrection. Surely a victorious body like Christ's, a body that has conquered sin and death, that has broken out of the grave with radiant new life, will be whole and without blemish? But not only is his body still scarred, it is those same wounds by which the disciples recognise Jesus, and they are overcome with joy.

Nor are these scars that are left over from a previous battle. They are not the cuts and bruises of a Hollywood hero who emerges victorious against impossible odds. They will not heal in time. These are the wounds of the cross. They are the terrible wounds of human betrayal, of torture, humiliation and degradation, and of an agonising death.

Were there other marks still on him? Was his nose still broken, his faced puffed and bruised from the beatings? Was his head still gashed from the thorns? We don't know. But those five scars – from the spear and the nails – have come to symbolise all Christ's earthly sufferings. And those are the marks found on the body of the risen, all-conquering, victorious Christ. The cross, it seems, has left Christ wounded for eternity.

Glorious scars

The risen Jesus was recognised by his scars. This story unites the resurrection with the cross: the one who has risen is the one who was crucified. Resurrection life never moves on from the cross as if it can be left behind – rather, it reveals the cross as a victory.

Resurrection life is none other than the way of the cross. Jesus makes this quite clear.

But John's story now goes further. It is the wounded and victorious Christ who gives the Holy Spirit to the Church. He breathes the Holy Spirit on the disciples and commissions them with the continuation of his own work. 'As the Father has sent me, I am sending you.'

This is where John tells of the gift of the Spirit. His picture of Pentecost contains what I would call a 'saving contradiction'. Pentecost, for John, is found in the place where the crucified, wounded one is recognised as the risen Lord.

By contrast Pentecostal and charismatic renewal movements in this century have tended to draw their theology of the cross and Pentecost through Luke's more linear, chronological account. This has often resulted in an unhelpful separation of cross and Pentecost, as if the Christian community leaves the former behind and 'moves on' into the latter (illustrated by the early use of two-stage language such as 'second blessing'). An understanding of renewal shaped by John's 'holistic' theology of cross, resurrection and Spirit will be less prey to insensitive triumphalism, more centred on the cross, and less easily distracted by the 'consolations' and manifestations that accompany the presence of the Spirit.[1]

In practice the struggle to hold together the 'saving contradiction' of cross and resurrection, defeat and victory, is too much for us. We end up emphasising one truth at the expense of the other. This is clearly revealed in Christian hymnbooks. There are large sections on the suffering and passion of Christ, and large sections on resurrection and ascension. But very few hymns attempt to bring the two together. It is disturbing to note that hardly any popular resurrection hymns celebrate the risen *and wounded* Christ. Rather, resurrection life is set in direct contrast to the life of earth and the suffering of the cross. 'The head that once was crowned with thorns, is crowned with glory now.'[2]

Almost alone of all the established hymn writers, Charles Wesley returns again and again to celebrate Christ risen and wounded. Central to his vision of the returning Christ at the end of time are the marks of the cross:

> Those dear tokens of his Passion
> Still his dazzling body bears,
> Cause of endless exultation
> To his ransomed worshippers:
> with what rapture,
> Gaze we on those glorious scars![3]

He is the exception, and many modern hymnbooks omit this verse. In popular devotion wounds and resurrection are kept clearly separate. At different times in the history and life of the Church we find one truth emphasised at the expense of the other.

God's visitation

In the church where I used to worship, there was a stained-glass window depicting Christ on the cross. The window was narrow, so the hanging figure looked strangely squeezed. He was thin and gaunt; his face was exhausted and lifeless. He actually looked like the victim of a long and debilitating illness rather than a crucifixion. The image was literally sickening.

But what made the window so striking was the fact that the local council had placed a neon street light on the road directly outside the window. At evensong during the winter months, the dying, emaciated body of Christ glowed down on us, bathing the congregation with a sickly shade of luminous green.

Where Christ's wounds are expressed in isolation from his resurrection, a particular view of human suffering emerges. The rediscovery of the healing, transforming work of Christ is still relatively recent. For the last four hundred years the Church of England has officially taught the faithful to expect the opposite. The *Book of Common Prayer* was quite explicit about this. In the liturgy for use when visiting the sick there are no prayers for healing – only for endurance and patience. The priest states quite categorically, 'whatsoever your sickness is, know you certainly, that it is God's visitation'. The sickness was God's 'fatherly correction', to add 'seriousness to his/her repentance'. The pastoral advice that followed included making a will![4] Where there is no expectation of the possibility that God might break in and heal, the only alternative is to invest that suffering with divine meaning. This view is still widely held among Christians, though never stated so starkly.

I was once asked to lead a discussion for a healing prayer group. In my talk I spoke about the risen Christ showing the disciples his wounds. I suggested that this was a source of hope in our own wounds. I tried to encourage a vision of the risen Christ ministering through the very things that leave us defeated, and leading us to new life and healing. I tried to speak of the possibility of the victory of Christ's love in and through our own wounds and struggles.

The discussion that followed was dominated by stories about people who were struggling courageously through terrible illness and tragedy. I had no reason to disbelieve them: the way people seem to manage through appalling adversity is fearfully moving, and a mark of God's grace. Yet although the group had asked me to speak about healing, they themselves spoke constantly about suffering. Devoted and caring though the members of that group were, I came to believe that they were deeply confused in their vision of the wounded and *victorious* Christ. In the end there was no hope of healing – only of redemptive suffering. The healing service that followed had the feel and expectancy of an intensive care ward.

The mystique of suffering

In such a context, the question Jesus once asked a blind beggar is very important. 'What do you want me to do for you?' (Mark 10:51). It may be that the risen, wounded Christ asks the same question.

In the Monty Python film *The Life of Brian*, there is a scene in which Brian passes a row of filthy beggars and cripples in a Jerusalem market. In the middle of them is an obviously healthy man in a brilliant white loincloth. He is calling out, 'Penny for an ex-leper.' He then complains loudly that he was making quite a good

living as a leper until someone called Jesus came along
and healed him.

The truth is that we can grow to love our wounds.
In a perverse way they become our source of security.
They set limits to our lives; we know where we are
with them. We can even safely complain about them!
They become the means by which we relate and estab-
lish our place in the community. A community that is
preoccupied by a perverse 'love' of its wounds is one
that will have no desire to grow. Strangely at home
with suffering, it will find any encounter with healing
and new life very disturbing. Ida Gorres writes, 'I'm
inclined to think that one root of the fascination of
the "mystique of suffering" is the peculiar fashion in
which it fuses charity . . . with the desire for power.'[5]

A body like yours

If the cross can be emphasised without resurrection,
resurrection can also be emphasised without the cross.

In a church located in the same city as the church I
referred to earlier was a quite different picture of
Christ. Here he was the risen and victorious Christ. He
was pictured as if sitting on an invisible throne, filling
the wide East window. One hand was raised in blessing, the other extended in a gesture of greeting or
instruction. His crowned head had blonde hair, and
deep blue eyes gazed down upon the church. His naked
body was powerfully muscular, radiantly handsome
and enviably fit. A red robe discreetly trailed across
his loins. There were no wounds upon him. Standing
demurely in the window of the Lady Chapel was a

very beautiful, unblemished, blue-eyed Virgin Mary, with long blonde hair. She was holding a beautiful, blonde-haired, blue-eyed baby boy.

This appalling confusion of muscularity for Christianity presents Christian life as an impossible ideal. Before that window I felt the same sense of inadequacy and hopelessness that I once experienced on a misguided visit to the gymnasium of a local health club. The Christ in that stained-glass window was already a creature remote from and beyond my own feeble humanity. His victory was unsurprising because he knew no human weakness. He was quite unmarked by any experience of this frail and violent world; he had left all that behind him. To be faithful to such a vision of Christ, the Church must exclude anything that contradicts it.

Faith based on such a vision leaves us in precisely the dilemma that made Jesus so angry with the institutional religion of his day. He felt passionately the injustice of religion that made impossible and condemning demands on people, while offering no support for those who tried to respond. 'Religion is very good at describing the vision from the mountain tops', said Rabbi Lionel Blue. 'It is never very good at telling us how to live in the valleys below.'

The age-old divisions of the Church have not helped either. Typifying a common suspicion among Protestants towards 'Catholic' devotions to Christ, a preacher I once heard criticised Christians who used crucifixes rather than empty crosses for their devotions. 'Christ is not still on the cross,' he argued. 'He has risen.' I remembered because I was struggling with depression at the time. Believing was very hard, but I had found no way of sharing my struggles with anyone in that church. The whole place felt so positive and full of resurrection that I felt I would be letting the side down. The only thing I knew then was that my cross was *not* empty, and I was being told that I was not welcome there.

This memory came back unbidden when I read of the British armed forces returning, victorious, from the Falklands war. The most wounded and disfigured soldiers were actually kept away from the press photographers. No sight of wounds was allowed to spoil the celebrations.

I have suggested that some Christian traditions can be trapped in a mistaken view of suffering that actually excludes the transforming power of resurrection life. But the hymns and songs of today's charismatic renewal movements in the Church, for all their vitality and vision, have yet to honour the wounds of the risen Lord. These wounds are needed to temper a disturbing enthusiasm for military language, for marching, winning victories and crushing evil.

The American preacher, Tony Campolo, made the same point in a different way when he warned that resurrection life (or 'life in the Spirit')

is not about having wonderful spiritual experiences of joy and worship, or speaking in tongues, victorious praying, or seeing dramatic healings and visions (though they have their place). To be filled with the Spirit is to have your heart broken by the same things that broke Jesus's heart.

Ultimately there is no resurrection that is not a resurrection out of hell.

It is the mark of a mature community of resurrection
that it can find room for the expression of pain and
struggle without the death of hope – and enter the
celebration of hope and victory without excluding or
neglecting those who still suffer. 'Rejoice with those
who rejoice,' wrote St Paul; 'mourn with those who
mourn' (Rom. 12:15).

It was in this spirit that Jean Vanier, founder of
the l'Arche communities, suggested that every act of
Christian celebration should include a a time of silence
to remember those who could not yet celebrate. In
such a place Christ can come and reveal himself as
companion in our wounds, while calling us into celebration of his victory.

Without shame

The vision of a wounded and risen Christ on Easter
day invites us to live more honestly with the wounds
we carry ourselves. Most of us choose not to, if we
can avoid it. John Goldingay has written very movingly
of the experience of sharing life and ministry with his
wife Ann, who suffers from multiple sclerosis. His
words always leave me responding with new understanding to the wounds of Jesus.

> When I go and speak at some conference, often the
> thing that people take away is not anything I have
> said but their meeting with Ann, though they rarely
> articulate what it is that has affected them. My guess

is that she embodies human characteristics which belong to us all but which we normally seek to evade, such as fragility, dependence and uncertainty. She brings these demons out into the open in such a way as they cease to be demons. Indeed, she reveals that they are angels. They are part of being human, part of the nakedness which humanity originally wore without shame, and they are therefore part of imaging God.[6]

Reflecting on how her illness has influenced his own life (as a theological college principal) he says:

I know in my own person that the disabled exercise an important ministry to the ordinary. [I have] institutional power which I can misuse, I can beat students in an argument most of the time if I choose to do so. Imagine what a so-and-so I might have been if it were not for the positive shaping effect on me of Ann's disability. I know she slows me down, for good. She makes me appreciate simple things, like squirrels, clouds and the swaying of the willow tree outside our house.

Ann's illness frees both tears and frustration, both love and anger, both resilience and guilty powerlessness. God does not organise, dominate, or do miracles for Ann. God lets her be. Perhaps she ministers to God.[7]

Saving wounds

If there are no marks on the risen Jesus, then resurrection is only for the unmarked. When we see him marked, we dare to celebrate that we may rise too.

The hope of resurrection is found precisely where
life most contradicts it. Long before resurrection is
concerned with any glorious *ascent* to the life of
heaven, it will first *descend* and embrace our wounds.
In fact there will be no resurrection without them. Our
renewal and transfiguring will begin from the place of
our deepest defeat and despair.

This is the only way of making sense of this appearance of Christ, with such love and purpose, to a broken
community, hiding behind locked doors for fear of the
outside world. In his wounds, they recognised their
own.

The wounds of Jesus are very significant for our
understanding of his ascension into heaven. In Luke's
gospel, where the ascension is the final resurrection
appearance, Jesus 'lifted up his hands and blessed them'
(Luke 24:50). These are the same scarred hands by
which the disciples had earlier come to recognise him.
He then ascends in the same glorified *and wounded*
body.

In the words of Simon Barrington Ward,[8] Jesus
becomes for us 'the Wounded Man in the heavens',
bearing in his own body the needs and longings of this
world before the Father's throne. It is the most fearful
hope of all that Christ calls us to rejoice in: that somewhere there is a place where our deepest struggles
with loss and brokenness are held in an embrace that
promises new life. And Christ in his resurrection, with
his glorious scars, is the pledge of our transfiguring too
– wounds and all.

On Easter night, during the vigil of resurrection,
there is an ancient symbolic ritual. Into the large

paschal candle at the front of the church, the priest presses five grains of incense and says these words:

— by his holy and glorious wounds, may Christ our Lord guard us and keep us.[9]

8 The marks of believing
Jesus and Thomas

Now Thomas (called Didymus), one of the Twelve, was not with the other disciples when Jesus came. So the other disciples told him, 'We have seen the Lord!'

But he said to them, 'Unless I see the nail marks in his hands and put my finger where the nails were, and put my hand into his side, I will not believe it.'

A week later his disciples were in the house again, and Thomas was with them. Though the doors were locked, Jesus came and stood among them and said, 'Peace be with you!' Then he said to Thomas, 'Put your finger here; see my hands. Reach out your hand and put it into my side. Stop doubting and believe.'

Thomas said to him, 'My Lord and my God!'

Then Jesus told him, 'Because you have seen me, you have believed; blessed are those who have not seen and yet have believed.'   (John 20:24–9)

Where was Thomas on the night that Jesus appeared to the disciples? Was he taking an urgent phone call? Had he popped out to collect a takeaway meal? We can imagine him returning with the food ('Five plaice and chips, seven cod and chips, two pasties and chips, three pancake rolls, and a large bottle of Diet Coke') to find everyone so overwhelmed and excited that no one is interested in eating.[1] Wherever Thomas had gone that evening he had left his friends behind locked doors, fearing the violence of the authorities and still deep in the trauma of the death of Jesus. He returned to find himself bombarded with astonishing stories of Jesus appearing to them. 'We have seen the Lord!'

How would you have felt? The shock must have been enormous.

Thomas is remembered for his doubts, but he might equally be remembered for his unfortunate timing. This is the man who managed to miss the resurrection!

True believer

Apart from this resurrection story Thomas makes only two other appearances in the gospels. We know very little about him.

We first meet him after Jesus had announced that he was returning to an area where only recently his life had been seriously threatened. When the disciples failed to change his mind, Thomas turned to the others and said, 'Let us also go, that we may die with him' (John 11:16). Whether this was meant sarcastically or out of misplaced bravado we don't know. But he shows no understanding of what Jesus is saying or doing.

On another occasion Jesus was preparing his followers for his coming 'departure' (the word he sometimes used to speak of his approaching death). He tells
them he is going to prepare a place for them. 'You
know the way to the place where I am going', he says.
Thomas bluntly contradicts this assumption. 'Lord, we
don't know where you are going, so how can we know
the way?' He is as confused as ever but his honesty –
and cheek? – are rewarded as he draws from Jesus one
of the most famous sayings he ever gave. 'I am the
way and the truth and the life. No-one comes to
the Father except through me' (John 14:1–6).

Taken together the three stories give us a picture of
a quite ordinary, unremarkable man. He is down to
earth, capable of large enthusiasms and great stubborn-
ness. He contributes no distinctive insights. Like his
fellow disciples he is easily confused by what he sees
and hears of Jesus. What stands out is his directness
and honesty. He had a quality that Graham Greene
always looked for in 'true believers': 'a certain capacity
for disloyalty'; a refusal to go along with the crowd or
to toe the line. This makes the true believer incapable
of committing atrocities. They would never be the sort
who would plead that they were 'just obeying orders'.[2]

Every community needs a character like Thomas
someone who is willing to ask the questions that no
one else dares to. Such people are truthful, and they
keep their friends more truthful too.

Doubt and faith

It is important to recognise that in this resurrection story Thomas in some way represents all the disciples. The gospels record that they *all* doubted the resurrection. Even at the very end of St Matthew's gospel, where Jesus met his eleven disciples on the mountain-top and commissioned them with the gospel, we read, 'When they saw him they worshipped him; but some doubted' (literally, 'drew back'; Matt. 28:17).

To illustrate something of their struggles to believe and trust in the risen Jesus, St John tells the story of one of them – Thomas. He intended the experience of Thomas to be a personal example of what they all wrestled with. The story is an encouragement and challenge to those who come after. The prayer for St Thomas' Day recognises this when it thanks God,

> who, for the firmer foundation of *our* faith,
> allowed the apostle Saint Thomas
>   to doubt the resurrection of your Son,
> 'til word and sight convinced him . . .' [my italics][3]

John began the story by reminding us that Thomas was a twin (the meaning of 'Didymus'). Whether he intended it or not, this has often been taken as a symbolic way of saying what this story is about – the relationship between doubt and faith in Christian life. They are twins.

If that is true then it is evident that this story has been much misused. How did the Church come to rename this disciple as '*Doubting* Thomas'? No gospel writer gave him that nickname. More to the point, it is not true: he believed. No other disciple has such a name; we don't speak of 'Peter the Denier' or 'Promiscuous Mary Magdalene'. So why has the Church persisted in naming this follower of Jesus as an unbeliever? What is it about doubting that the Christian community cannot forget or forgive?

'Faith means doubt,' insisted Thomas Merton, 'it is not the suppression of doubt. You overcome doubt by going through it. The man of faith who has never experienced doubt is not a man of faith.' But the popular Christian understanding of faith all too easily leaves us feeling that our doubts and questions are not acceptable. We must hide them. Doubt is seen as a lack of faith, as the opposite of believing. The tragedy of such a faith, however sincerely held, is that it has nothing to give us when we most need help.

'I know I shouldn't doubt and I should have faith but I do find it hard to understand what has happened and why God allowed it.' The speaker was a woman who was struggling to cope with a series of personal tragedies in her life. Her understanding of faith was clear and very sad. Faith meant accepting whatever happened to us. It meant being polite and respectful to God. It meant not complaining and not asking questions. And so, in the midst of her pain, anger and bewilderment, she could not share her struggles with God as she really needed to.

I can remember the precise moment when I could stomach that view no longer. I was sitting in a prayer meeting the morning after the Hillsborough football disaster in which ninety-four spectators were crushed to death. The mood was subdued. No one knew what to say. This disaster was only the latest in a long line of tragedies that had hit the news that autumn.

We bowed before God, weighed down with pain and unable to express it. A few prayers were offered but they felt pious and empty. We kept lapsing into silence. From the back a voice suddenly burst out, 'Lord, I just don't know what you're playing at. I don't know what you think you're doing. It's so hard to believe in you when things like this keep happening.'

Those words liberated something in me that day. I went home and told God exactly what I thought of him. I told him of the pain and shame of trying to speak of him in a world where such things happened. I confessed my fear that my faith would not be strong enough to survive a world like this.

Faith to doubt

I have since discovered that this kind of 'doubt' is held in very high esteem in the Bible. Living faith is marked by the willingness to question and even challenge God's ways. Doubting, questioning and even protesting are signs of a real relationship with God.

The people of the Old Testament speak to God with breathtaking directness. Utterly perplexed by God's dealings with him, Moses cries out, 'Why do you treat your servant so badly? In what respect have I failed to win your favour, for you to lay the burden of all these people on me?' (Num. 11:11 NJB). Many of the psalms address God with the same boldness. 'Answer me when I call to you, O my righteous God!' (Ps. 4:1).'Why, O LORD, do you reject me and hide your face from me?

... You have taken my companions and loved ones from me; the darkness is my closest friend' (Ps. 88:14, 18).

Abraham Heschel writes,

> the refusal to accept the harshness of God's ways in the name of his love was an authentic form of prayer. Indeed, the ancient Prophets of Israel were not in the habit of consenting to God's harsh judgment and did not simply nod, saying 'Thy will be done'. They often challenged him, as if to say, 'Thy will be changed'. They had often countered and even annulled divine decrees ... A man who lived by honesty could not be expected to suppress his anxiety when tormented by profound perplexity. He had to speak out audaciously. Man should never capitulate, even to the Lord.[4]

Henri Nouwen comments on these words:

> This attitude shows, in fact, how close the Jew, who can protest against God, feels to God. When I can only relate to God in terms of submission, I am much more distant from him than when I can question his decrees.[5]

Good doubt

The vitality and boldness of such relating to God is notably absent in much Christian spirituality.

When I first arrived in my present parish I planned an eight-week discussion series on Christian belief. I advertised it for non-Christians who wanted to discuss Christian faith without feeling pressurised. I offered it to those wanting to prepare for confirmation, and I also invited any who had been Christians for years but wanted a refresher course. I wasn't sure what to call it until I heard myself saying to the congregation, 'It's a kind of "Agnostics Anonymous"!'

The response was immediate, and over the next few years it was the most popular group in the church and attracted people of all ages and backgrounds. One of the comments I kept hearing was, 'I have been coming to church for years and I have never felt able to ask these questions before.'

I felt very nervous trying to lead those meetings. There was no predicting what questions would come up, and no guarantee we would find an answer we could take away. But the most exciting discovery was seeing how the freedom to question faith actually brought faith to life. We sometimes speak of acting in 'good faith'. We also need the possibility of living with 'good doubt'. The truth is that human nature is most fulfilled when it is questing and questioning. We are made to be explorers and searchers. And when we think we have found the answers, we grow dull and make our bed on them. I have long thought that Christian evangelism has overemphasised Jesus as 'the answer' to life. I know what is meant by the statement; but the picture of faith as finding an answer easily implies that something is complete and finished. That has never been my experience. Rather, Christ is the one in whom all life suddenly becomes infinitely greater, more costly, more glorious – and wonderfully alive to its God. 'God is the surprise of the universe, not the answer', wrote David Jenkins.

This was certainly our experience in those discussion

evenings. We sometimes stumbled home with more questions than we arrived with. We often struggled with confusion. Nor was everyone who came convinced. But we never lost the sense that God enjoyed those evenings too.

My Lord and my God

We do not know why Thomas doubted what his friends told him. Our doubts and questions are never simply intellectual issues. So many personal factors affect our freedom to trust, or need to question what we hear. Our whole experience of life – good and bad – is revealed in how we respond to new discoveries. In my experience, one of the factors that most inhibits people when faced with the challenge of new experience of God is the pain of having been let down before. Thomas may have been resentful that he had missed such a life-changing encounter; spiritual jealousy is much more common that we admit. I have always been one of the frustrated few people still standing up or *not* shaking at the end of dramatic charismatic meetings. And as I step over the bodies in the aisles and struggle past shaking prayer groups to reach the exit, feeling very left out, I wonder if this is how Thomas felt.

But this whole story is actually a wonderful and unexpected encouragement to those who find it hard to believe the way everyone else seems to. There is hope here for those who don't seem to share the experience that everyone else seems to have had.

There is a place for people who don't conform to the way the community of faith believes.

Jesus personally seeks out a doubter on the edge of the faith. Not only that, he agrees to Thomas's demands to examine and probe his wounds. But he brings to him a particular challenge – 'Stop doubting and believe.' The original Greek here expresses a fuller meaning: it could be translated 'Stop doubting *once and for all* and *keep on* believing.' Doubt, questioning and scepticism can become compulsive. Jesus is telling Thomas that he needs to come off the fence and commit himself one way or the other.

In the Bible, doubts and questions are never an excuse for avoiding commitment. 'I've got a lot of questions,' said a man I was visiting recently. I was there (at his wife's invitation) to discuss the baptism of his baby boy. He was explaining why he didn't come to church. At least *he* seemed to think it was an explanation. He sat there with a large glass of whisky, a successful businessman in a comfortable house. In the hall was a large bag of golf clubs and in the drive was an expensive car. Nothing wrong with any of that, of course, but he didn't look like a man deeply troubled by questions. He didn't seem to lack sleep. He certainly hadn't lost his appetite.

Real questions leave their mark on us. They haunt, irritate and disturb us. They give us no rest. They force us to get *more* involved with life, not less. Our doubts remind us of our frailty and lack of understanding. They humble us.

This is where true faith emerges from. 'It is not as a boy that I believe in Christ,' wrote Fyodor Dostoev-

sky, 'but my hosanna has passed through a great furnace of doubts'.[6] Doubts are not an excuse for laziness.

Faith and sight

Strangely, the one point in this story at which Thomas
appears to be criticised is at the very moment he
declares his faith. 'Because you have seen me, you have
believed,' said Jesus; 'blessed are those who have not
seen and yet have believed.' This is very good news
for the Christian generations who followed the era of
the first apostles and who never witnessed Christ in
human flesh. It is an easy temptation to assume that
believing must have been easier for people in the gospels than it is for us: Jesus warns against making that
mistake.

In fact it is clear that the sight of Jesus was never a
guarantee of faith. Many people saw Jesus and were
not convinced by him. One of the greatest paradoxes in
the gospels is the way that the 'ungodly', the 'sinners',
recognised the Son of God while the 'godly', 'religious'
people were unable to see who was before them. It
was a blind man who called out in faith and was
healed, while Jesus warned the watching Pharisees,
saying, 'If you were blind, you would not be guilty, but
since you say, "We can see," your guilt remains' (John
9:41 NJB).

Seeing is not believing. The decision to believe
involves an act of faith, as does the decision not to
believe. The 'life of faith' is not something only
religious people undertake. It is the only way we can
live in this world. I met someone at a party once who,

on discovering I was a Christian, told me he was an atheist. He said it with a finality that implied that we had nothing in common. 'So we're both believers,' I replied. He looked astonished and very disappointed.

Life itself requires constant acts of faith. I have no certainty that my car is perfectly safe before I drive it. I have no certain guarantee that the food I buy at the supermarket will not poison me. Everything I do requires this fundamental act of trust. And the more significant my choices, the greater is the uncertainty involved. How can two people ever know enough about each other to take all risk out of the decision to get married? And if daily living requires such trust and risk, how much more will we struggle to commit ourselves to God?

The poet R. S. Thomas expresses the pain of this dilemma for me. In 'The Waiting' he writes of the vulnerability of prayer that grows rather than lessens with the passing years:

> Young
> I pronounced you. Older
> I still do, but seldomer
> now, leaning far out
> over an immense depth, letting
> your name go and waiting,
> somewhere between faith and doubt,
> for echoes of its arrival.[7]

Leap of faith

After taking everything into account, after checking and rechecking and taking all possible advice, we are still left with no option. We must risk committing ourselves – to 'stop doubting and believe'. Or not.

Sheldon Vanauken described this dilemma as he struggled to decide whether to believe the Christian faith or not.

There is a gap between the probable and the proved. How was I to cross it? If I were to stake my whole life on the risen Christ, I wanted proof. I wanted certainty. I wanted to see him eat a bit of fish. I wanted letters of fire across the sky. I got none of these . . . It was a question of whether I was to accept him – *or reject*. My God! There was a gap *behind* me as well! Perhaps the leap to acceptance was a horrifying gamble – but what of the leap to rejection? There might be no certainty that Christ was God – but, by God, there was no certainty that he was not. This was not to be borne. I could not reject Jesus. There was only one thing to do once I had seen the gap behind me. I turned away from it, and flung myself over the gap towards Jesus.[8]

9 The far side
The restoration of Peter

Afterwards Jesus appeared again to his disciples, by
the Sea of Tiberias. It happened this way: Simon Peter,
Thomas (called Didymus), Nathanael from Cana in Galilee, the sons of Zebedee, and two other disciples were
together. 'I'm going out to fish,' Simon Peter told them,
and they said, 'We'll go with you.' So they went out and
got into the boat, but that night they caught nothing.

Early in the morning, Jesus stood on the shore, but
the disciples did not realise that it was Jesus.

He called out to them, 'Friends, haven't you any fish?'

'No,' they answered.

He said, 'Throw your net on the right side of the
boat and you will find some.' When they did, they
were unable to haul the net in because of the large
number of fish.

Then the disciple whom Jesus loved said to Peter,
'It is the Lord!' As soon as Simon Peter heard him

*say, 'It is the Lord,' he wrapped his outer garment
around him (for he had taken it off) and jumped into
the water. The other disciples followed in the boat . . .
When they landed, they saw a fire of burning coals
there with fish on it, and some bread.*

*. . . Jesus came, took the bread and gave it to them,
and did the same with the fish.*   (John 21:1–9, 13)

The story of Peter appears as an afterthought in John's
gospel. He clearly intended to finish his gospel at the
end of the previous chapter. There he told of the discovery of the empty tomb; of Jesus appearing to Mary
and giving her a message for the disciples; of Jesus
revealing himself to the disciples and commissioning
them in the Holy Spirit. Thomas' journey from doubt
to faith in Christ acts as a final parable, and John
concluded his gospel with a closing appeal to his read
ers – 'that you may believe that Jesus is the Christ, the
Son of God, and that by believing you may have life in
his name' (John 20:31).

Some time later, Chapter 21 was added   by John,
or by someone carefully following his style. The reason
may well have been popular demand: 'You can't finish
the gospel without telling us what happened to Peter!'

After these things

The story begins. The scene has changed from Chapter
20: the upper room in Jerusalem is now the shore of
the Sea of Galilee (also called Tiberias). Now the same
disciples who were joyful in the resurrection a few

verses before appear to be standing around wondering what to do next.

After the previous chapter we would have expected signs of new life and confidence among them, but the impression instead is one of drifting and restlessness. Peter, as always, takes the lead. He has more reason than most to want to leave recent events behind. 'I'm going fishing,' he says. And the others all join him.

It is a poignant moment. For three years they had followed an extraordinary man whom they had come to believe was God. They had left everything for him. Now their own lives have apparently gone full circle; for them, the story is over. The most natural instinct, in times of insecurity, is to go back to a place that feels familiar and secure. These disciples are going back to fishing.

Yet they catch nothing all night. The story is telling us something important here. It seems that not only are the disciples unable to enter new, risen life, they can find no way to re-enter their old life either. This is their dilemma: they are caught between two worlds, at home in neither. The scene is set for the third resurrection appearance.[1]

The charcoal fire

It is dawn, and in the early light the disciples see a man standing on the shore. They are forced to admit to him their nets are empty. He tells them to fish from the other side and suddenly their boat is almost sinking from the weight of fish. In that moment Jesus is recognised.

Peter impulsively leaps out of the boat to swim for

the shore – but not before he has first got dressed! Most people take their clothes *off* before swimming: Peter's need to cover himself before meeting Jesus is very significant.

There on the shore is a charcoal fire. The parallel is surely intentional. Only a few days ago, in the chill and half light of early dawn, Peter stood by a similar charcoal fire[2] and was asked if he was a follower of Jesus. There he denied it three times.

The disciples must have felt very awkward: Jesus has caught them deserting. Peter's actions throughout betray a man desperate to please.

Jesus, however, appears completely relaxed. He greets them from the shore like a friendly, hopeful customer – 'Haven't caught any fish, have you?' He then makes a gift of a miracle of fish so extravagant that it echoes his first miracle of wine at Cana (where Nathanael, among the group, came from).

When they stumble ashore Jesus offers them break-fast and serves them. It must have been a strange meal. I can imagine the disciples sitting tongue-tied and embarrassed, forcing themselves to eat out of pol-iteness. But Jesus is described taking and giving bread and fish in phrases deliberately chosen to remind the disciples both of the Last Supper and also of the wild generosity of the feeding of the five thousand.

The story moves on

When they had finished eating, Jesus said to Simon Peter, 'Simon son of John, do you truly love me more than these?'

'Yes, Lord,' he said, 'you know that I love you.'

Jesus said, 'Feed my lambs.'

Again Jesus said, 'Simon son of John, do you truly love me?'

He answered, 'Yes, Lord, you know that I love you.'

Jesus said, 'Take care of my sheep.'

The third time he said to him, 'Simon son of John, do you love me?'

Peter was hurt because Jesus asked him a third time, 'Do you love me?' He said, 'Lord, you know all things; you know that I love you.'

Jesus said, 'Feed my sheep.'   (John 21:15–17)

The story now focuses on one person. To be reconciled to the risen Jesus will be something all the disciples must struggle with. This is Peter's story. We know that Peter has witnessed the risen Jesus at least twice before, but now the other disciples withdraw and Peter is alone with him.

What was it like? So much had painfully come between them. Could Peter have expected Jesus to speak to him ever again after what he had done?

In Mark's resurrection account the angels give the women a message from Jesus for 'the disciples *and Peter*', telling them they will meet him in Galilee (Mark 16:7). We can only imagine what that personal note must have meant to Peter. But as Mark records that the women fled in terror and told no one, it may have been some time before Peter got the message at all.

By the charcoal fire, Peter is once again questioned three times about his allegiance to Jesus. Twice he replies defensively, 'You know I love you!' Is he really surprised that Jesus should have to ask?

The third time finally cuts through to him. He is hurt and he surely knows why. But he still has no way of admitting his need or confessing his betrayal. He still pleads in self-justification: 'You *know* that I love you.' He wants to be able to repair the damage and move on without having to go back and face what he actually did. Between the lines he is really pleading, 'Can't we just forget about what happened and start again?'

Re-membering

Peter has a difficult and painful journey to make. He will not be able to enter new life until he has first returned to what still lies buried and unreconciled in his past. Lovingly but firmly, that is where the repeated questions of Jesus lead him. There is no other way. 'Salvation does not bypass the history and memory of guilt, rather it builds upon it and from it.'[3]

Until there is a remembering there can be no forgiveness. To re-member means to put back together something that has been broken and dis-connected. This means more than recalling an event or action from the past; it is not a feat of memory. The opposite of remembering is not forgetting: it is *dis*-membering.

To truly remember requires that we turn back to past actions or relationships and recognise our own place within what happened – perhaps for the first time. Only there can reconciliation be offered and received. Rowan Williams writes that there can be no healing or restoration 'until the memory itself is exposed, and exposed as a wound, a loss. The word of forgiveness is not audible for the one who has not "turned" to his or her past'.[4]

There is nothing more painful than a relationship so broken by mistrust or pain that even gestures of reconciliation and caring are interpreted as further evidence of treachery and just make matters worse. For a relationship to be restored there must be a willingness to turn to one another, and that always means facing our place in the cause of the pain. Anyone who has struggled to 'get it right' in seeking a reconciliation where the anger and wounds are deep knows the risk that Jesus took with Peter. Peter could so easily have refused to face it at all. He could have lost his temper and walked away.

Dis-membering

Memories of the horrors of the last war have been reawakened by a series of poignant anniversaries in recent years, and particularly memories of the liberation of the concentration camps. In the trials that followed the war it was apparent that many of the Nazi commandants who had supervised the death camps had somehow 'neutralised' the memory of what they had done. Adolf Eichmann, for example, presented himself in court as a tidy civil servant, on top of his paperwork, proud of meeting his quotas and his schedules. He appeared untroubled by the fact that his work was the attempted annihilation of an entire race. He seemed to suffer from no guilt or anxiety. His memory bore no relation to the horrors in which he had participated.

The trial of Eichmann, in 1961, was even more disturbing for the fact that psychiatrists had examined him and pronounced him perfectly sane! It was this that provoked Thomas Merton to write his brilliant meditation on Eichmann's trial. By declaring Eichmann 'sane', said Merton, the whole civilised world was revealing that it suffered from the same problem. A civilisation that can pronounce a mass murderer sane has lost hold of its own sanity. Eichmann was therefore found to be part of a whole culture that was refusing to turn back and properly to remember the terrors it was part of. Merton's warning was stark:

> The whole concept of sanity in a society where spiritual values have lost their meaning is itself meaningless. We can no longer assume that because a man is 'sane', he is therefore in his 'right mind'. If he were a little less sane, a little more doubtful, a little more aware of his absurdities and contradictions, perhaps there might be a possibility of his survival . . .[5]

Participation

While I was visiting the United States a few years ago an American friend spoke of the struggle in her society to come to terms with the Vietnam war. She told of the overwhelming temptation to hide from the disaster that it became, by stressing the heroism, sacrifice and moral ideals of those who fought there.

My friend took me to the Vietnam Memorial in

Washington DC. Its design continues to cause great controversy, and I could understand why: it was unlike any memorial I had ever seen before. Traditional war memorials *uplift* the names and the memory of those who died. This tendency is stronger in Britain, where war memorials are usually also monuments to victory. Memory is not therefore readily associated with defeat.

The Vietnam Memorial is not a monument at all. You don't look up, you look down. You do not stand before it, still and silent – you enter it and participate. A path has been cut into the side of a small hill. It slopes gently down and up again alongside a wall of black marble on which the names of the dead and missing are engraved in endless columns. I watched two young women trace a name from the wall – perhaps their father. A man was seen weeping and beating his fists against the wall in his grief. By inviting participation it both confronted and healed. It was place to re-member.

I found the experience overwhelming. Unlike traditional memorials, there was no separation between those who died and those who now remembered. There was no separation from the wounds of death and death's meaning. Even as a foreigner, with no personal experience of war, I found myself led down into the dark wounds of recent history. There was no safe distance from which to observe and stay safely detached: by inviting participation it was a place that both confronted and healed.

Returning

Memory alone cannot save us. It may just as easily break or overwhelm us. If there are some who can shut out all remembrance, there are many who long to forget and cannot. 'Fifty years – and I've never left the place,' wept a Jewish survivor on her recent return to Auschwitz.

Another survivor of a concentration camp was Corrie ten Boom. She toured Germany after the war, preaching the need for forgiveness and reconciliation. After one meeting a man approached her. She was horrified to recognise him as one of the cruellest of the camp guards. He had since become a Christian. He asked from her the same forgiveness he had received from Christ. His hand was outstretched waiting. Memories of his violence flooded back and she froze at the thought. But she had always taught that forgiveness is first of all an act of will and obedience to Christ. She prayed:

> Jesus, help me! I can lift my hand. I can do that much. You supply the feeling   And so woodenly, mechanically, I thrust my hand into the one stretched out to me. And as I did, an incredible thing took place. The current started in my shoulder, raced down my arm, sprang into our joined hands. And this healing warmth seemed to flood my whole being, bringing tears to my eyes. 'I forgive you, brother,' I cried. 'With all my heart.'[6]

There is a danger in telling dramatic stories in this context, for real forgiveness is very costly and we all struggle with it in different ways. For some the moment of release and healing may be quite sudden. For many others the call to re-member remains painful and requires continual prayer and compassion, like tending a deep wound that is slow to heal and needs regular rebinding and cleansing. This is why Christian liturgy always includes prayers of penitence, forgiveness and absolution: these are partly so that we may receive cleansing for our wounded nature and hear again of the hope of final healing.

I recall a seminar on the healing of memories in which the speaker shared the lifelong pain he had carried because of his treatment as a child by his parents. Very simply and undramatically he told how, for the last thirty years, he had daily prayed words of forgiveness for his parents and sought the love, mercy and healing of Christ for those memories.

In the light of all this we begin to recognise the compassion with which Jesus ministers to Peter. Jesus accompanies Peter back into the memory of his most terrible failure and betrayal, and so into his deepest self. There by the charcoal fire, he waits to meet him again, for only there can Peter be forgiven and restored. The most loving gift Jesus can offer Peter is to lead him to the place where he faces his true self, and be there himself when he arrives. Rowan Williams suggests that the primary ministry of the risen Jesus is precisely this – to give us back our memories. What we forget, leave behind, deny or simply cannot face by ourselves, he holds in living remembrance until we can come to a place where we can receive it back.

What Christ did for Peter, he works constantly to do for us also.

The wound of love

Peter's deepest encounter in this story was not with himself, his awfulness, sin and guilt. It was with divine love. It was love that sought him, not judgement. Love had led him to this place. With love Jesus now commissions him in service again. 'On the far side of resurrection, vocation and forgiveness occur together, always and inseparably'.[7] The real burden of Christ's forgiveness is that it leaves us struggling with the knowledge that we are loved without condition. Although it is the news we most long to hear, nothing in our lives ever quite prepares us for this place and the reality is frightening to us. Not surprisingly, someone once called the experience of forgiveness the 'hell of mercy'.

Like Peter, when we come to the place of our true memory, of our sins and our capacity for darkness, our greatest struggle will not be with sin, evil or judgement. It will be with goodness, with the terrifying and joyful wonder of being loved by God.

In *The Lord of the Rings*, the Company of the Ring have narrowly avoided disaster and have been resting in the healing enchantment of the beauty of the woods of Lorien, in the care of the beautiful Elf Queen. All too soon, the time comes to resume the journey. As they leave, Gimli the Dwarf weeps his grief at leaving such a place of love and healing.

'Why did I come on this Quest? Little did I know where the chief peril lay! Torment in the dark was the danger I feared, and it did not hold me back. But I would not have come, had I known the danger of light and joy. Now I have taken my worst wound in this parting. Alas!'[8]

'To have opted for love', wrote Brother Roger of Taizé, 'is to open yourself to a wound from which you never recover.'

> God of terror and joy,
> you arise to shake the earth.
> Open our graves
> and give us back our past;
> so that all that has been buried
> may be freed and forgiven,
> and our lives may return to you
> through the risen Christ, Amen.[9]

10   What is that to you?

A postscript

'Why do you look for the living among the dead?'

(Luke 24:5)

We do not come to risen life naturally. If we did, we would have found it long ago. Risen life is the gift of Jesus, who of his own free, unfathomable choice, desires to seek us out and bring us home.

The great encouragement of the first resurrection community was that it was made up of such an unpromising group of people. None of them came to it naturally. They were grief-stricken, fearful, theologically confused, full of doubts and prejudices, locked away from the world, or planning to return to their old way of life. And that is where Jesus came and met each one of them. Each encounter, each word and action, lovingly fitted to the one before him.

The good news of resurrection lies in this very contradiction. This is the work of the risen Christ. And if he so carefully and patiently pursues such improbable people, he surely seeks us too.

Between the momentous cosmic events of Easter, Ascension and Pentecost, these brief, unexpected stories of the resurrection appearances give us hope where we would not otherwise dare to look for it. For it is here that we find ourselves, too: somewhere between death and resurrection, seeking the dead yet puzzling over rumours of life. And this is where Jesus will find us, and our remaking will be just as improbable and unexpected.

High up in the archway of the North entrance of Chartres Cathedral is a carving called 'The Creation of Adam'. God is sitting beside the figure of Adam, who has emerged as far as his waist from the dust of the earth. Adam is leaning against God, resting his head on his lap, his right hand clutching God's knee. He looks exhausted with the effort of being created. Perhaps he is asleep. Perhaps he has yet to receive breath at all.

With his right hand God supports Adam's head, while his left hand is poised over him as if about to stroke his hair. They could also be the hands of a potter over the clay.

God's head is upright. His eyes (perhaps from the effect of years of weathering) appear closed. The mood is of intense care and concentration. Yet I fancy there is joy welling just beneath the stone surface: God creates with the ease and passion of one for whom such work is life itself. There is no hurry. He has all eternity.

How long has that hand been poised over Adam?
For what does God wait? But nothing will distract him
from completing what he has begun.

Notes

Introduction

1. David Runcorn, *Touch Wood* (DLT, 1992).
2. Quoted in Pauline Warner, *Women's Icons of Ministry*, Pastoral Series no. 60 (Grove, 1994), p. 11.
3, 4. Both phrases from a passage of C. S. Lewis's comment on the writing of Charles Williams. In the context of the chapters that follow, the passage is worth quoting in full:

> Christians naturally think more often of what the world has inflicted on the saints; but the saints also inflict much on the world. Mixed with the cry of martyrs, the cry of nature wounded by Grace, also ascends – and presumably to heaven ... [Williams] had no belief in a conception of Grace which simply abolishes nature; and he felt that there was always something legitimate in the protests of nature against the harrowing operation of conversion.

> Quoted in Simon Tugwell, *Reflections on the Beatitudes* (DLT, 1980), p. 67.

1   A door has cracked open

1. Stephen Davis, *Risen Indeed – making sense of the resurrection* (SPCK, 1994), p. 168. Much of the thinking in this chapter has been influenced by this very helpful study.
2. Philip Seddon, *Darkness*, Spirituality Series no. 5 (Grove, 1983), p. 3.
3. Reviewing a book on New Testament spirituality written from within the Evangelical tradition, Philip Seddon comments on the same evident unease. Concluding an otherwise positive survey of the book, he notes 'the usual anti-mystical thrust recurs . . . The expositional approach dominates over the exploratory, the informational over the reflective, the didactic over the demonstrative.' *Anvil – an Anglican Evangelical journal for theology and mission*, vol 12/no. 2 (1995), p. 181.
4. From the third Eucharistic prayer in the *Alternative Service Book* (Clowes/SPCK/Cambridge, 1980), p. 137.
5. Davis, p. 184.
6. If the resurrection and the empty tomb are denied as historic events, it is not clear what basis Liberal theologians find for speaking of spiritual resurrection instead. They appear to be insisting on the spiritual reality of an event they claim did not happen. The arguments are well reviewed in Davis, Chapters 3 and 4. For a recent collection of studies on the resurrection from the Liberal standpoint, see Stephen Barton and Graham Stanton (eds), *Resurrection: essays in honour of Leslie Houlden* (SPCK, 1995).
7. This dualistic belief has found popular expression in the meditation 'Death is nothing at all' by Henry Scott Holland, which is often requested as a reading at funeral services:

    Death is nothing at all . . . I have only slipped away

into the next room. I am I and you are you. Whatever
we were to each other that we are still. Call me by
my old familiar name, speak to me in the easy way
which you always used. Put no difference in your
tone; wear no forced air of solemnity or sorrow. Laugh
as we always laughed at the little jokes we enjoyed
together. Play, smile, think of me, pray for me. Let
my name be ever the household word that it always
was. Let it be spoken without effort, without the
ghost of a shadow on it. Life means all that it ever
meant. It is the same as it ever was; there is absolute
unbroken continuity. Why should I be out of mind
because I am out of sight? I am waiting for you, for
an interval, somewhere very near, just around the
corner. All is well.

(Quoted in James Bentley, Andrew Best and Jackie Hunt
(eds), *Funerals – A Guide* (Hodder & Stoughton, 1994),
no. 425.) It is a difficult request to refuse in such circumstances, but though parts of the reading include very
helpful advice on grieving, the philosophy behind it
represents a serious distortion of Christian hope in the
face of death. Holland treats the fact of death as something negligible. The departed tells the mourners, 'I have
only slipped away into the next room. . . . Life means
all that it ever meant . . . there is absolute unbroken
continuity.' That these words were written by a Canon
of St Paul's Cathedral has lent false authority to ideas
about death, body and spirit that are nowhere found in
the Bible. Far from trivialising death as an 'insignificant'
or 'negligible accident' (as some popular versions state),
death is an enemy. Nor did Jesus brush it aside. He
confronted it, descended into the hell of it, and defeated
it in his own body.

8. Davis, p. 30.
9. Tom Stoppard, *Arcadia* (Faber & Faber, 1993), pp. 47–8.

10. Michael Bordeaux, *Risen Indeed – lessons in faith from the USSR* (DLT, 1983), pp. 41–2.
11. The story is told in Mary Craig, *Candles in the Dark – six modern martyrs* (Hodder & Stoughton, 1984), p. 164.
12. David Runcorn, *Touch Wood* (DLT, 1992), p. 132.
13. Davis, p. 10.
14. Charles Handy, *The Age of Unreason* (Arrow Books, 1990), pp. 4ff.
15. The poem is my own.

2 Loving the space between

1. Metropolitan Anthony Bloom, *School for Prayer* (DLT, 1970), Chapter 1.
2. I have written more fully about aspects of this time in *Space for God* (DLT, 1990).
3. Nico Kazantzakis, *Zorba the Greek* (Faber, 1980), p. 125.
4. Quoted in Alan Jones, *Soul Making* (SCM, 1986), p. 122.
5. Kahlil Gibran, *The Prophet* (Heinemann/Pan, 1980), p. 16.
6. Quoted in a personal letter from a friend. Source unknown.
7. Quoted in Andrew Louth, *The Wilderness of God* (DLT, 1991), p. 151.

3 Why are you weeping?

1. See John Richards, *Tears – A Gift of the Spirit?*, a study paper published by Anglican Renewal Ministries. See also the wonderful study of tears: Maggie Ross, *The Fountain and the Furnace – the way of tears and fire* (Paulist Press, 1987), pp. 243ff.
2. Notable exceptions are Alan Jones, *Soul Making* (SCM, 1986), Chapter 4, and Richard Foster, *Prayer* (Hodder & Stoughton, 1994), Chapter 4.
3. Ross, p. 238.

4. Ibid., p. 10.

5. Ibid., p. 138.

6. Simon Tugwell, *Reflections on the Beatitudes* (DLT, 1980), p. 67.

7. Ibid., p. 65.

8. Ibid., p. 61.

9. Ross, p. 14.

10. By an unknown monk of the 13th century. Quoted in André Louf, *Teach us to Pray* (DLT, 1978), p. 38.

11. *The Complete Poems of Cecil Day-Lewis* (Sinclair-Stevenson, 1992), p. 546. For an extended reflection on this theme see John V. Taylor, *The Christlike God* (SCM, 1992), Chapter 7, on the cost of creation.

12. J. R. R. Tolkein (Unwin, 1978), p. 990.

4 Stranger on the road

1. Mark Stibbe, *John – Readings: a new Bible commentary* (Sheffield Academic Press, 1993), pp. 13–14.

2. Walter Brueggemann, *Hopeful Imagination – prophetic voices in exile* (SCM, 1986), p. 71.

3. David Runcorn, *Space for God* (DLT, 1990), pp. 68–9.

4. Erich Fromm, quoted in Kenneth Leech, *True God* (Sheldon Press, 1985), p. 183.

5. Kenneth Leech, *The Eye of the Storm – spiritual resources for the pursuit of justice* (DLT, 1992), pp. 220–1.

6. This is the practice where psalms are arranged for public worship.

7. Josh McDowell, *Evidence that Demands a Verdict* (Here's Life Publishers, 1986), p. 144.

8. G. B. Caird, *Luke* (Penguin, 1963), pp. 258–9. This brief commentary is unusual in discussing how Jesus may have approached the Old Testament in this story. Most other commentaries leave the question unanswered.

9. Rowan Williams, *Open to Judgement – sermons and addresses* (DLT, 1994), pp. 158–9.
10. Printed on a prayer card. I have been unable to trace the source.

5 Some of our women amazed us

1. Franco Zeffirelli (director), *Jesus of Nazareth* (1977, distrib. ITC Entertainments Ltd). Transcribed from soundtrack.
2. Alan Ecclestone, *Scaffolding of the Spirit* (DLT, 1987), p. 74.
3. Jane Martin Soskice in Andrew Walker (ed.), *Different Gospels* (SPCK, 1993), pp. 198–9.
4. Quoted in Charles Elliott, *Praying the Kingdom* (DLT, 1985), p. 32.
5. James Nelson, *The Intimate Connection – male sexuality, masculine spirituality* (SPCK, 1992). A fascinating study.
6. George Carey, 'Women and authority in the Scriptures' in Monica Furlong (ed.), *Feminine in the Church* (SPCK, 1984). Carey writes (p. 48), 'It is the nature of Scripture, after all, that under the Holy Spirit new insights and fresh understandings are discovered in different generations'.
7. Discussed in Kenneth Bailey, 'Women in the New Testament: a Middle Eastern cultural view' in *Anvil* vol. 11/no. 1 (1994), pp. 11–12. This study makes a very important contribution to the understanding of women in the Church of the New Testament.
8. See Bailey (pp. 15ff.), for example, on the cultural background to Paul's teaching concerning women in the Church at Ephesus.
9. Ecclestone, p. 64.

10. 'Leader Comment', *The Independent*, 15 October 1993. See also 'Leader Comment', 12 February 1995.

11. *Alternative Service Book* (Clowes/SPCK/Cambridge, 1980), p. 246.

12. James Nelson, *The Intimate Connection – male sexuality, masculine spirituality* (SPCK, 1992), p. 17.

13. See Monica Furlong, *A Dangerous Delight – women and power in the Church* (SPCK, 1991), summarised in Chapter 7.

6 It's flesh I'm talking about here!

1. James Morrow, *Towing Jehovah* (Granada, 1994).

2. Helen Lemmel, 'Turn your eyes upon Jesus', in *Junior Praise* (Marshall Pickering, 1986), no. 260.

3. James Nelson, *The Intimate Connection – male sexuality, masculine spirituality* (SPCK, 1992), p. 23.

4. The word that medieval theologians used to describe the special abilities of Jesus's resurrection body.

5. Quoted in Raymond Brown, *The Gospel According to John*, vol. 2, XIII-XXI (Geoffrey Chapman, 1972), p. 990.

6. C. S. Lewis develops this idea in his fantasy *The Great Divorce* (Fontana, 1974).

7. I believe the phrase should be attributed to Rowan Williams. The theme underlies his wonderful study *Resurrection* (DLT, 1982). See also Chapter 16 of my *Touch Wood:* 'A kind of love affair'.

8. Rubem Alves, *I Believe in the Resurrection of the Body* (Fortress Press, 1984), pp. 7–8.

9. Ibid., p. 9.

10. Sister Margaret Magdalene, *Transformed by Love* (DLT, 1989), p. 8.

11. Toni Morrison, *Beloved* (Picador, 1987), pp. 88–9. I have also drawn on an article on Toni Morrison by Mandy

Russell-Jones in *Leading Light – Journal of the C. S. Lewis Centre*, vol. 1 (3 March 1994).

7 The wounds that keep us

1. For a more extended discussion of this issue, see Tom Smail's very helpful contribution in Andrew Walker, Nigel Wright and Tom Smail, *Charismatic Renewal – The search for a theology* (C. S. Lewis Study Centre/SPCK, 1993), Part 2, Chapter 4 'The cross and the Spirit – towards a theology of renewal'.
2. Thomas Kelly, 'The head that once was crowned with thorns', in *Mission Praise* (Marshall Pickering, 1990), no. 647.
3. Charles Wesley, 'Lo! He comes with clouds descending', in *Anglican Hymn Book* (Church Society, 1966), no. 81.
4. 'The Order for the Visitation of the Sick', in *Book of Common Prayer* (Cambridge University Press, 1964), p. 312.
5. Quoted in Rowan Williams, *Resurrection* (DLT, 1982), p. 28.
6. Quoted by kind permission from *St John's Theological College Newsletter*, no. 61 (December 1993). Goldingay reflects further on this theme in a subsequent newsletter, no. 65 (April 1995).
7. Ibid.
8. Simon Barrington Ward, *Love Will Out* (Marshall Pickering, 1988), p. 33.
9. 'The Easter Liturgy', in *Lent, Holy Week and Easter Services and Prayers* (Church House Publishing/Cambridge University Press/SPCK, 1984), p. 229.

8 The marks of believing

1. I have 'borrowed' this picture from a sermon by Simon Jenkins.
2. Discussed more fully in Alan Jones, *Soul Making* (SCM, 1986), pp. 118–19.
3. *Alternative Service Book* (SPCK/Clowes/Cambridge, 1980), p. 785.
4. Quoted in Henri Nouwen, *Genesee Diary* (Image Books, 1981), p. 142.
5. Ibid.
6. Quoted in Roger Pooley and Philip Seddon (eds), *Lord of the Journey* (Collins, 1986), p. 401.
7. R. S. Thomas, 'Waiting', in *Later Poems 1972–1982* (Macmillan, 1983), p. 111.
8. Sheldon Vanauken, *Severe Mercy* (Hodder, 1977), p. 98.

9 The far side

1. I refer to John 21:14. John appears to be counting appearances to *groups* rather than individuals at this point.
2. The Greek word *anthrakian* (charcoal fire) is the same in both instances, and only appears in the gospel on these two occasions.
3. Rowan Williams, *Resurrection* (DLT, 1982), p. 34.
4. Ibid., p. 21.
5. Thomas Merton, 'A devout meditation on the trial of Adolf Eichmann', in *On Peace* (Mowbray, 1976), pp. 82ff.
6. Quoted in Richard Rice-Oxley, *Forgiveness – the way of peace*, Ethical Series no. 75 (Grove, 1989), p. 16.
7. Williams, p. 35.
8. J. R. R. Tolkien, *The Lord of the Rings* (Unwin, 1978), p. 399.
9. Collect for Easter Day in Janet Morley, *All Desires Known* (SPCK, 1992), p. 14.